running well

running well

Sam Murphy and Sarah Connors

HUMAN KINETICS

Library of Congress Cataloging-in-Publication Data

Murphy, Sam.
  Running well / Sam Murphy & Sarah Connors.
      p. cm.
  Includes index.
  ISBN-13: 978-0-7360-7745-3 (soft cover)
  ISBN-10: 0-7360-7745-6 (soft cover)
  1. Running. I. Connors, Sarah, 1969- II. Title.
  GV1061.M877 2009
  796.42--dc22
                                    2008015021

ISBN-10: 0-7360-7745-6
ISBN-13: 978-0-7360-7745-3

First published in North America in 2009 by Human Kinetics, Inc.
First published in Great Britain in 2008 by Kyle Cathie Ltd.

The Web addresses cited in this text were current as of May 2008.

Acquisitions editor: Laurel Plotzke
Project editor: Caroline Taggart
Managing editor: Cory Weber
Designer: Geoff Hayes
Illustrations: Anne Wadmore
Copy editor: Ruth Baldwin
Editorial assistance and picture research: Vicki Murrell
Production: Sha Huxtable
Index: Alex Corrin

Color separations by Scanhouse Malaysia
Printed in China

10 9 8 7 6 5 4 3 2

Human Kinetics books are available at special discounts for bulk purchase. Special editions or book excerpts
can also be created to specification. For details, contact the Special Sales Manager at Human Kinetics.

Human Kinetics
Web site: www.HumanKinetics.com

United States: Human Kinetics
P.O. Box 5076
Champaign, IL 61825-5076
800-747-4457
e-mail: humank@hkusa.com

Canada: Human Kinetics
475 Devonshire Road Unit 100
Windsor, ON N8Y 2L5
800-465-7301 (in Canada only)
e-mail: info@hkcanada.com

contents

Acknowledgments

Sam Murphy and Sarah Connors would like to thank Mark Rowlands, UK Athletics Endurance Coach, Dr Sharon Dixon, senior lecturer in sport science at Exeter University, Ron McCulloch, a podiatrist and podiatric surgeon, and Karen Reid, a sports nutritionist, for their useful insights and feedback on the text.

Thanks also to The Runner's Shop in Beckenham and to ASICS for providing kit and footwear for our models. (The ASICS shoes shown in the book are the GEL–NIMBUS VIII for women and the GEL–1120 for men – see Resources section for stockists). And special thanks to the models themselves, Eleanor, Andy, Tom and Rachel.

Photographic credits

foreword

I was an international athlete for 12 years, running in three Olympic Games, three Commonwealth Games and many other major championships and international competitions. I won 12 major medals, eventually winning my two golds at the 2004 Olympic Games in Athens. During that time, and especially in the run-up to the Athens Olympics and beyond, it sometimes seemed to me that I was always suffering from one injury or other (that was how I got to know Sarah, one of the authors of this book). I had many different injuries, in particular a recurrent Achilles tendon injury that eventually played a part in my decision to retire.

Being a professional athlete is immensely stressful, particularly on the body, and the pressure to perform is enormous. Injuries don't help and I know about them only too well. But they are something that every athlete, at whatever level, seems to face. Many of us think that this is just something we have to put up with – and of course you can be unlucky. Nevertheless, there is a lot you can do to lessen the risk of serious injury. Understanding how your joints and muscles work is a great help in developing good technique, posture and strength, which in turn helps prevent injury and, when injuries do happen, get yourself back on track as quickly as possible. Of course, proper training (including knowing when to give yourself some time off) is vital, whether you are running once a week in the park or aiming for the next Olympic Games. This is what *Running Well* is all about. This is a great book and there is plenty of really useful information here for everyone. I feel sure it will help lots of people to "Run Well."

Dame Kelly Holmes

introduction

Nothing beats the pure, simple pleasure of running – a fact that an ever-growing number of devotees can attest to. Approximately 100,000 people applied for a coveted place in the 2007 New York City Marathon, while over two million women have now taken part in the UK's Race for Life series of 5K runs.

It's fantastic that so many people are choosing to get fit on their own two feet, but studies show that, in any given year, up to 70 percent of runners sustain an injury serious enough to stop them temporarily in their tracks. Even more worrying, many people believe injury is par for the course. But far from being an occupational hazard, running injuries are usually down to errors in training and technique. In fact, research suggests that simple mistakes – like wearing the wrong shoes, increasing mileage too quickly or not varying your sessions enough – are responsible for as many as 60 percent of running injuries, and a bigger factor than faulty biomechanics. It may not seem like it when you are laid up with an icepack on your knee, but this is good news, because it means that, with a little know-how and the right approach, problems can be avoided.

And that's where *Running Well* comes in – your ultimate guide to running well and staying injury-free. By learning the difference between training and straining, varying your speed and surfaces, choosing the right footwear, keeping the running muscles strong and supple, and honing – or even changing – your technique, you can minimize your risk of injury and the training setbacks it inevitably brings.

And if you are unlucky enough to get hurt, this book should still be your first port of call. Chapter 10 offers a comprehensive guide to more than 30 running injuries to help you get back on track as soon as possible. Helping you identify the problem and its possible causes, *Running Well* shows you how to minimize the damage and get the right kind of treatment and rehabilitation to prevent the injury from occurring again.

Discovering the secrets of injury prevention will not only save you physical therapy fees, pain, hassle and lost training hours, it will also help improve your running performance. How? Well, one of the key factors in improvement is consistent training – and nothing messes that up more than a constantly painful knee, a sore back or an inflamed Achilles . . . Learn how to keep injuries at bay and you'll see your running progress in leaps and bounds: the best reward of all.

chapter 1

top form

how to assess and improve your running technique

You may not need to be taught how to run, but, as the old saying goes, "It ain't what you do, it's the way that you do it," and it's certainly true that good running technique is a factor in injury prevention. But is there such a thing as perfect running technique? On paper, perhaps. In reality, probably not.

Perfect motion

Physical therapists and podiatrists can talk until they are blue in the face about the mechanics of the running gait – how the foot strikes, what muscles engage at what point in the proceedings and how the various forces are absorbed – but the fact is that only a tiny percentage of people, if put on a treadmill and observed, achieve textbook perfection and are able to put the theory into practice. What's more, opinions on what constitutes correct technique vary enormously. Some experts believe a heel strike is most natural, while others (such as Russian running coach Nicholas Romanov) maintain that this is a complete no-no and recommend landing on the forefoot, and still others say you should simply run in whatever way feels right for you. So, rather than striving for perfection, perhaps a more realistic aim is to achieve your optimal running form – the one that works best for you, given your natural physique, experience and fitness level and personal running style. When we say works "best," we mean in terms of comfort, performance and minimal risk of injury. And while that certainly allows for individual differences, there is some common ground as far as "good" technique is concerned.

CHEST
Keep the chest open. Think up and forward, as if you had a string tied to your sternum (breastbone), drawing you forward. But don't bend forward from the waist.

TORSO
While opinions vary on whether you should be upright or adopting a slight forward lean when running, you certainly don't want to be (a) leaning backward or (b) bending forward from the waist or hips. Keep your lower tummy gently pulled in.

WRISTS AND HANDS
Keep your wrists and hands relaxed. They don't have to be floppy – you can even maintain a very loose fist – but don't hold them rigid.

PELVIS
Picture the pelvis as a full bucket. If you tip it forward, backward or sideways, you'll spill its contents, so you need to keep it as level as possible. Being able to do this requires a combination of strength and flexibility. A pelvis that is tilted too far forward (an anterior tilt) is often associated with tight or sore lower back muscles, overactive hamstrings and a tight iliotibial band (see page 137). This posture can cause increased strain on the lumbar discs and facet joints, so it's imperative to work on strengthening the core and stretching out tight areas.

KNEES
Runners – and hecklers of runners – often say, "knees up," but lifting the knees up in front results in a wasteful bouncing motion. The knee lift is about driving the leg forward, not up. A bent knee has less resistance to rotation than a straight one, so the knee bend allows the leg to swing through more efficiently from the hip.

FEET
What part of the foot strikes the ground will depend on your personal technique. It may be the heel, the midfoot, or the ball of the foot. At touchdown point, you want your foot directly under your center of gravity. Don't clench your toes inside your shoes while running, nor deliberately spring off the toes as your foot leaves the ground.

HEAD

If you had to carry a 3–4.5 kg ball around all day, it would be a real drag, huh? Well, the bad news is, you do – your head. Given such a heavy appendage to contend with, how you hold it becomes remarkably important. If you crane your neck forward, or pull your head back, you'll put undue stress and strain on one side of the joints of the cervical spine (neck and upper back). You want it to be perfectly aligned above the vertebrae in the neck so that the weight is evenly distributed. Looking down is another no-no as the weight of the head coming forward throws the spine out of alignment. Your eyes should be looking ahead at the ground between 10 m and 30 m in front of you. Keep your jaw and neck relaxed, too.

SHOULDERS

Let your shoulders hang loose: hunched, tight shoulders waste energy and restrict your movement. Allow a slight rotation of the shoulder girdle around the spine – this is quite natural and counterbalances the rotation of the hips.

ARMS

It's remarkable how many different takes on arm position you see in runners. There's the circular motion, the side-to-side motion, and then there's no arm movement at all (a pity, because they do contribute to forward motion). Imagine your arms are pistons, firing you forward, with elbows bent somewhere close to 90 degrees and moving in a forward–backward direction, or just slightly across the torso. Moving your arms faster makes your legs move faster, so use more arm power when you're running hard, less when you're jogging. But don't try too hard – the effort needs to come only when you're bringing the arm back; it'll come forward on its own.

ANKLES

Don't run with rigid, flexed ankles. Let all the tension go when the foot is in the air.

HIPS

Relying too much on the quads and hip flexors rather than using the hamstrings and gluteals to extend the hips will reduce the power and length of your stride. Visualize rolling your hips underneath you so your bottom isn't sticking out. Running with your hips forward will help improve your knee drive effortlessly.

LOWER LEGS

Allow your lower leg to "dangle" below the knee when the leg swings through, rather than holding it out rigid. This feels a lot less strained and prevents overstriding. Contrary to popular belief, the calf muscles are not most active in the toe-off phase in aiding propulsion, but just as the foot lands, helping to decelerate the leg.

Step by step

Let's now take a closer look at what happens, or what should happen, in the running gait. The running gait or "cycle" is divided into two main phases: the "swing" phase, when the foot is in the air, and the shorter "stance" phase, when the foot is on the ground. When you are running at a relaxed pace, ground contact time is approximately .2 seconds, while "flight" time is .5 seconds. There's a brief moment when both feet are in the air, as one comes down to land just after the other has taken off.

When the foot lands (commonly, though not always, on the outside of the heel), it rolls slightly inward and forward, and the arch of the foot flattens to help dissipate the impact (this is the "pronation" bit we all hear so much about). It's worth reflecting on this for a moment, because pronation is often talked about as if it is a running "fault," when actually it is a perfectly normal part of the running gait. It's only when the foot pronates too quickly or too much that it becomes a problem.

Back to the gait cycle then: as the foot lands, the knee bends – muscles in the thigh and calf working eccentrically (lengthening) to decelerate you – while the opposite leg pulls through, the body passing over the supporting foot to roll off the toes (known as "toe-off"). The weight of the swing leg provides the momentum for you to move your body forward, aided by the muscle power of the calves and hamstrings, which facilitate the push-off into the next stride, and by the complementary action of the arms pumping. Just before push-off, the foot rolls outward into a "supinated" position, in which the arch stiffens to give greater leverage.

Individual differences

That's the overall picture, but, as we know, there are individual differences in terms of where on the foot you land, how far and how quickly the foot pronates on landing, how much propulsion there is in the toe-off phase, and how much hip extension and knee flexion there is. This is where the argument about whether you should try to change your running technique comes in. Some experts believe "If it ain't broke, don't fix it," while others feel that you should work to reach as close to the ideal as you can. We would suggest that if you feel comfortable and relaxed when you run, leave things as they are. If you are constantly injured, or find running a painful ordeal, consider working on changing your running technique. Changing it how, though? Well, first, you need to find out what you're doing wrong.

HIGH Q

The Q angle is the angle between the pull of the quadriceps from the kneecap to the crest of the pelvis. A higher Q angle is associated with wider hips and is more commonly seen in women. While the evidence is mixed, some studies have shown a link between a high Q angle and injury risk, especially problems related to the lateral side (outside) of the legs, such as iliotibial band syndrome and anterior knee pain.

The seven deadly sins of running technique

Some errors, such as looking down at the ground or clenching your fists, are easy to spot and remedy, while others take a bit more time to define – and change. The most common technique faults, and how to spot them, are outlined below.

1 Overstriding

Overstriding is literally trying to make your stride too big, putting the muscles in an inefficient lengthened position, and causing the foot to land in front of the knee, which creates a braking effect. Overstriding usually happens when you are "trying too hard" to run faster. Runners naturally tend to run at the stride length that is the most economical for them – in other words, the one that uses the least amount of oxygen for that speed. Overstriding is counter-productive, because it's less economical and requires more oxygen.

Do I do it? You will feel as if you are landing very heavily, and your ground contact time will be a little too long. If you could see yourself running from the side, your foot would strike the ground way out in front of your knee.

2 Wasteful movement

Since the overall direction of running is forward, too much up-and-down movement is a waste of energy. There's a story about a coach who used to have his runners run behind a hedge and he'd tell them off if he could see their heads bobbing above the top of the hedge! The most likely cause of a bobbing action is lifting the knees too high up in front and pushing off the toes. A very short stride can also be to blame. Poor arm action is another form of wasted movement: arms that are going across the torso are hampering forward motion.

Do I do it? You – or others – will have noticed a bobbing action as you run. You may feel more as if you are running on the spot than moving forward. You could also be susceptible to calf tightness or injury problems. As far as the arms are concerned, you may find you are always elbowing people in races, as your elbows splay out to the side instead of traveling forward and back.

3 Overpronation

As we've seen, pronation is a normal part of the gait cycle. It's only when the foot overpronates that there's a problem. This is because the foot attempts to push off while it is still "floppy" and the arch is still

collapsed, setting off a whole chain of bad affairs. For a start, this foot position puts extra stress on the muscles supporting the arch, which in turn pull on their attachments to the inside of the shin bone. The knee then rolls in and the iliotibial band (see page 137) becomes tight, pulling on its attachment to the patella (kneecap) and potentially causing anterior knee pain. Further up the body, the gluteals are put in an inefficient position by the inward rotation of the knees and don't work properly, causing tightness in the hip flexors and back and an anterior pelvic tilt.

Do I do it? Stand face-on to a mirror, in a relaxed stance. Are your kneecaps facing directly forward, or turning in ("squinting")? Now bend your knees and see what happens. The knees should travel down in a straight line and not roll inward. Rolling in indicates overpronation, which causes overload on the knee structures. Also try the wet footprint test on pages 44–45 to identify overpronation.

4 Sitting in the bucket

A posture in which the pelvis is tilted forward and the hips pushed back (often accompanied by a forward lean from the waist) is sometimes described as "sitting in the bucket," or sitting on the hips. This posture reduces the power of the hip extensors (the hamstrings and glutes), stresses the lower back and shortens your stride. It's often a result of weak muscles in the core (especially the glutes) and of poor pelvic alignment and tight hip flexors, though it can simply set in as a result of fatigue during a run. This posture is responsible for a lot of runners' back and hip problems.

Do I do it? One way of checking whether you are sitting in the bucket is to see whether you are able to roll the hips forward and tuck your pelvis under, slightly flattening the arch in your lower back. If you can, you were probably in a slight sitting position. If you see yourself running from the side and are a "sitter," you'd probably see an excessive arch in the lumbar spine, a protruding bottom and a low stride (which is sometimes "noisy"). Slack bum muscles are another tell-tale sign!

5 Excessive supination

Far less common than overpronation is oversupination – when, instead of rolling in too far, the foot doesn't roll in enough and actually remains on the outside edge. This reduces the foot's ability to absorb the shock of impact and increases the risk of stress fractures, especially along the outside edge of the foot and the shin. It also overstresses the connective tissues on the lateral side (outside) of the legs, such as the iliotibial band and a hip muscle called the tensor fasciae latae. Runners who oversupinate need a well-cushioned pair of shoes (see pages 46–47 for more advice).

Do I do it? This gait fault is more common among people with bow legs and high arches. A good test is to stand with bare feet and see if you can roll your feet in. If you don't have the mobility to do this, you may be an oversupinator. Also try the wet footprint test on pages 44–45. Oversupinators often have signs of excessive wear on the lateral side of their shoes.

6 Poor hip drive

Relying too much on the quads and hip flexors rather than using the hamstrings and gluteals to extend the hips reduces the power and length of your stride. A study in the journal *Strength and Conditioning Research* found that strengthening the glutes and hamstrings successfully improved running technique.

Do I do it? If there isn't much "action" behind the body – in other words, if your legs neither lift up very high nor bend very much behind you – you aren't getting full use of the power of extension and probably have very tight quads and hip flexors, and weak hip extensors.

Test Stand side-on to a wall to hold for balance and swing one leg freely, forward and backward, keeping it straight and relaxed. There should be a good back swing as well as forward. You may have poor hip drive if the pelvis feels "jammed," or if the swing leg splays outward on the back swing or the back appears to arch a lot (which means your body is trying to get extra range by cheating!). Work on

stretching the quads and hip flexors, strengthening the extensors and improving pelvic stability and mobility. (You'll learn more about all of these later in the book.)

7 Hip drop (Trendelenberg gait)

A pelvis that shifts too far from side to side produces something known as the Trendelenberg gait. As a result of weak adductors and abductors, the hip of the swing leg drops and the hip of the stance leg "pops out" to the side, because the muscles aren't able to hold the pelvis level. This makes the foot land in an incorrect position and can cause problems in the lower back and along the outside of the leg, especially with the iliotibial band.

Do I do it? Your hips drop from side to side as you run, like a catwalk model! From behind, your torso may also rotate toward the swing leg as you run.

Exercise To correct hip drop, try standing leg lifts. Stand side-on on a step with one leg hanging over the edge. Now "hitch" or lift the hanging leg so it's higher than the step, imagining that you are drawing the hip right up into its socket. Lower and repeat ten times. Also try the crab walk exercise on page 80.

SARAH'S CASEBOOK

The fabulously named malicious malalignment syndrome (MMS) is a combination of internally rotated thighbones, squinting patellae (kneecaps), externally rotated tibias (shin bones) and flat feet – which demonstrates perfectly how technique problems tend not to exist in isolation. I am the unfortunate sufferer of such a condition, which is probably what got me into physical therapy many years ago! The good news, though, is that it is possible to run with MMS. I manage it by wearing orthotics (tailor-made insoles) and stable trainers, and by being vigilant about stretching and core stability training.

How to run better

So are you guilty of committing any of these technique sins? Well, the good news is there are plenty of things you can do to improve your running style, both in terms of making simple adjustments to your body position and in making longer-term changes to your posture, strength, core stability and flexibility. Technique faults can be divided into two types: "intrinsic" (causes from within), such as bowed or "bandy" legs or poor core stability, and "extrinsic" (external), such as overstriding or leaning forward from the waist. It's much easier to correct extrinsic factors, as often these are simply habits or errors we aren't even aware of. But both types of problem can be corrected, or minimized to some degree, by following some of the tips in this chapter and with the use of stretches, strengthening exercises and drills included in this book.

Even if your technique leaves a lot to be desired, don't despair! It doesn't necessarily follow that you will suffer with injuries. Go to any race and you'll see runners with the most remarkable gaits trotting, shuffling and bouncing along quite happily! This just goes to show how amazingly well the body can adapt to – and compensate for – its biomechanical imperfections.

Relax

There's one easy step that we can all take to improve our running. And that's to be more relaxed. If you are frowning with concentration, trying to land on a specific point of your foot on every stride or pushing yourself beyond your limits, you'll be tense and won't enjoy your run or get the most out of it. This was demonstrated in a study in which athletes were asked to run a time trial at 110 percent of their maximum heart rate. The trial was repeated a few days later, and the runners were asked to work at 95 percent. As it transpired, all the runners were quicker when they ran at 95 percent, showing that trying too hard doesn't always get the desired results.

So what does running relaxed mean? Simply avoid tension and effort where it's not needed. For example, you don't need tense shoulders, clenched fists or a clenched jaw to aid your performance! If you tire very quickly when you run, or end up with neck or shoulder strain, you are almost certainly harboring unnecessary tension. Focusing on your breathing – perhaps counting to two as you breathe in and two as you breathe out – can help you stay relaxed. A good way of checking if you are harboring tension is to do a "body scan." This simply means taking a mental tour of your body, checking for any tension or stiffness and letting it go, or, if necessary, stopping to stretch out. Running relaxed, incidentally, doesn't mean running slowly – it is something you should be able to maintain whatever your pace.

Know the drill

One of the best ways to hone your technique is to practice some running drills. While they're par for the course for track athletes, road runners don't normally bother – but there's a lot to be gained from them. The purpose is to isolate and exaggerate a specific aspect of the running gait to perfect it before "putting it back in." Over time, this improves your coordination, range of movement and running technique as well as helping you to maximize your stride length and frequency.

Try the following five drills when you are thoroughly warmed up but still fresh. Start with 30 m initially, and gradually increase to 60 m as you become more used to them. Repeat each one three times. Begin with one session per week and, if you have time, add some drills to the end of a run, or introduce a second session.

TAKING GOOD TECHNIQUE IN YOUR STRIDE

Your running speed is determined by two things: your stride rate (number of strides per minute) and stride length. A typical runner's stride rate is 80–90 per minute (that's 160–180 steps per minute). So will taking bigger steps or more of them make you faster? Not necessarily. In experiments in which runners are asked to run at their preferred "comfortable" stride length, and are then asked to increase or decrease their stride, their effort level and energy expenditure go up. It seems that each of us has a preferred natural stride length for a given speed, and trying to change it forcibly may be counterproductive. The best way to enhance your stride is to stay strong and flexible (which you'll learn more about later in this book), work on the technique pointers in this chapter and try some running drills.

High knees
What? Walk forward, lifting the knee high and going on to the toes, holding for a second before moving to the other leg. Watch that you don't lean back or start tilting the pelvis, and keep the foot pulled up close to your bottom on the leg you are lifting.

Why? Good for core strength and balance, emphasizes the knee lift action needed for running.

Crossovers
What? Walk sideways, crossing one leg in front of the other, then go back the other way, with the opposite leg going in front. As you are able, increase the speed.

Why? This is great for balance and coordination and for waking up some of the non-running muscles.

Bottom kicks
What? Place your hands behind your buttocks and spring forward from foot to foot at a swift pace, kicking the heels back to touch each hand.

Why? This improves the speed of leg turnover.

Fast feet
What? Take small, fast steps forward, with minimal knee lift. Imagine the road is burning hot!

Why? This is good for reducing the contact time with the ground – the longer your foot stays on the ground, the more slowly you will run.

Backward walking

What? Slowly walk backward (ensuring you have a clear path). You can make this harder by taking the foot across the midline of your body as you are walking.

Why? This encourages the glutes to fire and is great to do before a speed session.

Don't run yourself ragged

Even those runners who *do* sometimes achieve textbook perfection with their running technique don't maintain that perfection 100 percent of the time. Fatigue comes in many guises. One elite 2:20 marathon runner reports that when he gets tired, his head goes back, which compromises his breathing and throws his center of gravity backward. Then there's the classic bobbing head of Paula Radcliffe. If you watch the end of a race, you'll see flailing limbs, dragging feet and dropped hips: all of this extra movement puts additional strain on the body. In light of this, give yourself plenty of recovery between sessions and avoid running – or drills – when you are too fatigued. For more advice, turn to page 58.

Get analyzed

If you've had recurring injury problems, it's worth investing in gait analysis at a podiatric or sports injuries clinic. A good gait assessment practitioner will not just tell you how you run, but also suggest ways of improving your technique, advise on specific strengthening and stretching work you need to do, and possibly recommend particular shoes or orthotics.

The session starts with a consultation about your running habits, including your mileage, shoes and surfaces, your stretching regimen, how long you've been a runner and any injuries or problems you've had. It can be useful to take your training journal with you, if you keep one.

Then the practitioner will do a "static" analysis – in other words, look at you stationary. He or she is looking at your general posture as well as things like knock knees, flat feet and any asymmetry between left and right, such as a leg length discrepancy or a wonky pelvis. They will also assess your range of movement in the relevant joints. Next, you'll be marked up with little sticky pointers at strategic points, such as the heels and pelvis, and hop on the treadmill to be filmed walking and running, from behind and from the side. This footage is then analyzed (either visually or using software, or both) and feedback given.

Remember to take your running shoes with you (take an old pair, too, if you are running in very new trainers that haven't yet taken on your "wear" pattern) and ideally wear bike shorts and a crop top so that as much can be seen as possible. Look in the back of running magazines for gait analysis.

So, we've talked about how to run. Now let's look at what we should be doing before and after those runs, in order to enhance the running experience and minimize injury risk.

chapter 2

gearing up and winding down

how to warm up and cool down effectively

You wouldn't catch any self-respecting elite athlete setting off for a run without a warm-up, but it's something the rest of us are frequently guilty of. In our busy, time-crunched lives, we believe that spending precious minutes limbering up for a run is a waste of time. Let us assure you, it is not!

While the scientific evidence on the benefits of stretching is mixed (as you'll see in the next chapter), the benefits of warming up prior to exercise have been well demonstrated in research studies. For example, a study in the *Journal of Orthopaedic and Sports Physiotherapy* found that a warm-up performed at 60 percent of maximal effort resulted in a 6 percent improvement in aerobic performance and a 7 percent improvement in anaerobic performance. Other research, from the University of Strathclyde in Glasgow, showed that intense exercise preceded by a warm-up resulted in less accumulation of blood and muscle lactate. Yet another study, this time from Manhattan College in New York, revealed that just five minutes of warming up enabled runners to exercise for longer than those who launched straight in. And, perhaps most important of all, a review in the journal *Physician and Sports Medicine* concluded that warming up reduces the risk of injury.

So far, so convincing. But what does a warm-up actually do? Well, it has a number of functions; most crucially, however, it raises body temperature and heart rate.

A higher body temperature is important for two main reasons. First, the chemical reactions involved in the release of energy occur more quickly in a warmer environment. For example, hemoglobin, the oxygen-carrying molecule in the blood, releases its oxygen to your hungry muscle cells more readily at higher temperatures. Second, warmer muscles and connective tissues are more pliable and less susceptible to injury, according to a study in the *American Journal of Sports Medicine*. The warm-up also prepares the joints for running by mobilizing and lubricating them. Articular cartilage, which cushions joint surfaces, does not have a blood supply, but relies on nutrients being delivered by synovial fluid. Movement makes this fluid less "sticky," and squeezes it into the joint capsule, allowing it to soak the cartilage and provide a protective cushion.

As for raising the heart rate, this increases blood flow to the working muscles, bringing them fresh oxygen and nutrients and removing metabolic waste products. At rest, muscles receive only about 15 percent of the blood circulating around the body. During vigorous exercise, like running, this increases to as much as 80 percent of total blood flow. Trying to run at speed without a prior warm-up doesn't allow time for the body to reroute all this blood, so your muscles are not able to work as efficiently.

Warming up might even make you run better. By enhancing neuromuscular pathways (the link between the muscular and nervous systems), warming up can increase the speed and efficiency of muscular contraction. This is particularly the case if the movements in your warm-up match the activity that you are about to do, suggests research in *Sports Medicine*.

maximum was found to be optimal, but a study on cyclists found that both high- and low-intensity warm-ups worked better than no warm-up at all in improving performance.

As a general rule, a warm-up should be at least five minutes long and could be as long as 20 minutes. If you are doing a short, fast session or race, the warm-up should be longer and more thorough than if you are embarking on a slower, more prolonged run. This is partly because you don't want to spend valuable time getting up to speed in a shorter session, but also because faster running and racing puts you at greater risk of injury. You should also spend longer warming up if it's freezing cold outside, or if you run first thing in the morning, when body temperature is lower.

Don't allow too much time to pass between completing the warm-up and beginning the activity – otherwise the benefits will be lost. And as far as the length and intensity are concerned, make sure that your warm-up doesn't leave you in a fatigued state – otherwise it will hinder, rather than help, your running.

How to warm up for running

All in all, then, a simple and not-too-time-consuming warm-up is likely to make your running experience better. So how do you do it? Well, there are three stages: First, mobilizing the joints to prepare them for movement; second, gentle but progressive aerobic activity to start to raise heart rate and body temperature and increase circulation; and third, running-specific movements to prime the brain and neuromuscular pathways. To be effective, a warm-up should be intense enough to cause mild sweating, which indicates that the body's core temperature has increased by about 2°F. Then you know the muscles will be ready for action. In a study published in the *Journal of Science and Medicine in Sport*, a warm-up that increased heart rate to 74–86 percent of

STRETCHING AS PART OF YOUR WARM-UP

The jury is decidedly still out on whether it's a good idea to stretch prior to exercise. You can read more about this in chapter 3, but a recent study from Monash University in Australia suggests that some pre-exercise stretching is worth it if you're already sore from a previous workout. In the study, stiffness and soreness of muscles, brought on by repeated muscle contractions 24 hours before, were reduced as a result of a stretching prior to a subsequent bout of exercise. The bottom line? If you're feeling a bit delicate, be diligent about your warm-up and consider including a few gentle stretches.

The warm-up: stage 1 – mobilization

Start with some gentle all-body movements, such as circling and bending and extending the joints to prepare the body for movement. Although running is a lower-body activity, it's important to warm up and mobilize all your body's major joints to prevent carrying tension and tightness with you. And remember, the aim of mobilizing is to take joints through their full range, not to attempt to *extend* their range. Perform the following sequence gently and rhythmically.

1 Take your ear toward your shoulder, keeping the opposite shoulder relaxed, and then move the head from side to side eight times.

2 Now bring your shoulders up toward your ears and roll them backward and down again. Repeat eight times.

3 Keeping your hips square, gently twist the upper body from one side to the other, looking over your shoulder as you do so. Repeat eight times.

4 Slide your hand down the outside of your thigh as you take the body to the side. Keep your hips in the center. Alternate from side to side, eight times.

5 Draw a large imaginary circle with the hips: rest your hands on your hips and take the pelvis as far to the side, back, other side and front as you can, keeping legs straight but not locked. Do four circles in one direction and then four in the other.

6 Pull one knee gently up to the chest, release, and lift the other knee. Do eight alternate lifts, and, on the final lift on each side, circle the ankle four times in each direction.

7 Finish by dropping your head to your chest and rolling down through your spine, with knees slightly bent and tummy tight, until you reach the ground. Pause, then roll back up, "rebuilding" the spinal column, vertebra by vertebra.

The warm-up: stage 2 – raising heart rate

Now begin to raise your heart rate by walking, either on the spot or forward, stepping up and down a stair, cycling or using a cross-trainer or stair-climber. Gradually increase your speed and range of movement, breaking into a slow jog if you are walking, over a period of 5–8 minutes. This gives your cardiovascular and musculoskeletal systems a chance to "change gear" and prepare for the activity to come.

The warm-up: stage 3 – running-specific activity

If you want to stretch as part of your warm-up, this is the time to do it, after a few minutes of general movement. (Find more information on stretching in the next chapter.) If not, it's time to add some running-specific stuff to wake up those neuromuscular pathways. This is a great time to incorporate some of the drills from pages 19–21, or try the two exercises below and opposite. You can even make this final stage of the warm-up session-specific – for example, by jogging some slow hills if you are doing a hill session, or adding some "strides" if you are doing a track session. Strides are a slightly slower version of a sprint: from a standing start, begin to run and gradually accelerate to a pace just below your sprint speed. Go for 5 x 20 m.

Prone kicks

Prone (face-down) kicks are a great runner's warm-up. The knee joint isn't put through its full range of motion during running, which means that parts of the joint capsule don't get fed with synovial fluid. This exercise feeds and lubricates the entire joint surface of the knee without impact. Lie on your front with your head resting on your hands, your tummy gently pulled in and your pelvis

level. Start slowly kicking alternate heels up to your bum, making sure the foot travels all the way back to the floor between kicks and that your pelvis stays still. As you continue, speed the movement up, and add some repetitions in which you lower the leg slowly but bring it up quickly. Aim for 1–2 minutes, or count 120 kicks.

Hamstring swings
Prone to hamstring pulls or tears? According to *Running Research News*, this exercise puts the hip through a full range of movement with no impact and warms up the hamstrings. Stand side-on to a support, and, with your knee bent, lift the leg to hip height and swing it up, down and back in a circular motion, the leg almost fully extended at the end of the backswing. Do 20 on each leg, increasing the range and speed with each one but always maintaining control.

How to cool down

So your run is over. What are you going to do? If you are like most runners, stop your watch and hit the shower! But finishing your run with a cool-down is a far better idea. While there is less evidence to support cooling down than there is to support warming up, it makes logical sense not to stop suddenly after a run, but to slow down gradually – the same way you started. If you've been doing a vigorous session, such as speed work or a race, you'll know how dizzy and unsteady on your feet you can feel at the end of the run. This is because blood is rushing around the body at top speed and is suddenly not needed any more, causing it to pool in the limbs, lowering blood pressure and often causing feelings of giddiness or nausea.

Once you've finished your session, spend a few minutes jogging slowly before breaking into a walk in order to allow your body's systems to return part way back to normal. A study from Japan shows that the heart rate recovers more quickly with a six-minute cool-down than with complete seated rest, while research in *Physiology of Sport and Exercise* shows that blood lactate is removed more quickly during active recovery, compared to rest, because blood flow remains elevated for longer.

Another study, from Atlanta, found that a cool-down enhanced the overall exercise experience, perhaps because it gives you time to ponder over your achievements and enjoy a feeling of accomplishment. Just as with the warm-up, the intensity at which you've been exercising dictates the length of the cool-down. If you've just done a steady run, it won't take you so long to get back to a resting state, compared to a punishing threshold session, for example.

Now you have cooled down and recovered, but your muscles are still warm – it's the perfect time to stretch. This window of opportunity lasts about 20–30 minutes, so you have time to take a shower, grab a snack and change into something comfy first if you want to.

freedom of movement

the lowdown on flexibility and stretching

Stretching isn't exactly a laugh a minute. It's tedious, uncomfortable and time-consuming. So why do we do it? And should we care if we don't? Read on before you draw your conclusions – and keep a flexible mind . . .

Before we start, an important point about terminology. Stretching is the method we use to maintain or enhance flexibility. And flexibility isn't just about lengthening muscles; it's also about taking joints through their full range of motion and increasing blood and nutrient supply, which is important for keeping cartilage nourished and healthy, reducing stiffness and maintaining correct musculoskeletal alignment.

Will it make me faster?

But will working on your flexibility help you become a better runner? Or a less injury-prone one? The scientists still don't know. For every study that shows one thing, another research project finds the opposite to be true. There is even some evidence to suggest that stretching can negatively affect endurance running performance – specifically running economy and power output. The study, published in the *International Journal of Sports Medicine*, found that in a group of runners, the least flexible ones (indicated by sit-and-reach test performance) had the best running economy. In other words, they were able to run at a given speed at a lower percentage of their maximum effort. But other research contests that it is only when stretching is performed immediately prior to exercise that it has a

negative (and temporary) effect on running economy and power. In a study from Scandinavia in which subjects stretched for 10 weeks, three days a week, they improved their flexibility without any detrimental effect on their running performance. Meanwhile, other research suggests that increasing hip flexion and extension, through flexibility training, reduces aerobic demand – making for improved performance.

It's tricky to compare studies, because each one uses subjects of different age, gender and ability, different types of stretching and different time periods. But here are a few of the conclusions that can be drawn:

● There is no evidence that stretching immediately prior to running has an effect on injury prevention.
● There is some evidence that stretching immediately prior to running has a negative effect on performance.
● There is evidence that regular stretching, performed daily, can be beneficial to health.
● Stretching does not appear to reduce subsequent muscle soreness from exercise.
● There is some evidence to suggest that better flexibility leads to better running performance. And some that it leads to worse running performance.

The case for stretching

Given all this, you would be quite within your rights to decide that there isn't enough conclusive evidence on stretching and that you are going to ditch it, or continue to neglect it. But we think that that's a bad idea! The trouble is, because many of us dislike it, we don't spend enough time or effort on stretching and then it doesn't work – reinforcing our belief that it's a waste of time. However, doing it properly may result in a very different experience. To understand why, you need to know a little about what stretching does.

So what happens when you stretch? When you first take, say, your calf muscle, into a stretch, muscle "spindles" located among the muscle fibers detect a change in the muscle's length and report back to the spinal cord. The nervous system sends a message to the nerves governing these fibers to tell the muscle to contract, in order to take it out of the stretched position. This is known as the "stretch reflex."

However, if the stretch is maintained for more than a few seconds (which, in many a runner's case, it is not!), another, more sophisticated receptor, located where the muscle attaches to the tendon and called a Golgi tendon organ, comes into play. This receptor can detect not only changes in the length of the muscle but also in the amount of tension it holds. So, hold that stretch and the Golgi tendon organ, noting that the muscle fibers are contracting and lengthening, triggers a reflex relaxation of the muscle (via a process called autogenic inhibition) to protect the muscle from damage. This is why easing into a stretch slowly and then holding it allows the muscle to relax and lengthen.

Over time, stretching can increase the length of the muscle, or at least maintain it at – or restore it to – its optimal functioning length. But why does this matter?

Well, running, as you probably realize, involves repeated contractions of specific muscles over a long period of time. This can leave the muscle fibers shorter in length than normal, and misaligned (like hair that needs combing). Stretching is the process we use to restore muscles to their resting length and realign these fibers. Without it, we risk them shortening permanently (by a process called adaptive shortening) and, in doing so, altering the function of the joints they are connected to. For example, if the hip flexors (which work very hard in running) tighten and shorten, they pull the front of the pelvis down and throw the lower back out of alignment, which can have all sorts of knock-on effects.

SARAH'S CASEBOOK

If you have had an injury to a muscle, stretch the area on a daily basis after the first 48 hours have passed. If you do it any sooner, the wound won't have healed and further bleeding will occur.

● Muscular balance, body awareness and posture are enhanced.
● Stretching helps to flush out metabolic waste products post-run.
● It gives you time out to relax and reflect on your session.

When to do it
When – and how often – should you stretch? Ideally every day, suggests research in the *Clinical Journal of Sports Medicine*, which found increases in both muscle force and power in subjects who stretched daily for several weeks. The benefits ranged from 2 to 5 percent improvement, which, they estimated, could make the difference to an elite athlete between winning a gold and not making the podium at all – small, but worthwhile, gains. Another study showed that running speed improved as a result of regular stretching when it was not performed immediately prior to exercise, but this was in sprinters, so may not be so relevant to distance runners. Even more important than the possibility of shaving a few seconds off your time is the possible reduction in injury risk. While it is now widely believed that there is no evidence that stretching reduces injury risk, this refers to stretching pre-workout, as part of a warm-up, not as a separate regular practice. Three studies have found a significant decrease in injury risk as a result of regular stretching – or, to put it more accurately, as a result of good flexibility.

What's more, flexibility naturally declines as we age if we don't maintain it – and changes take place in muscle fibers and connective tissue. Collagen fibers within the connective tissue thicken and, without regular stretching, get stiffer. Soft tissue becomes more dehydrated, decreasing joint lubrication and causing creakiness. One study concluded that stiffness and lack of flexibility were more a result of lack of use than of age per se, while another – on ageing runners – found that stride length declined primarily as a result of decreased range of motion at the hips and knees. Range of motion at the knees during running decreased by 33 percent and at the hips by 38 percent between the ages of 35 and 90.

So, while we can't categorically say that stretching will reduce injury risk or improve performance, it will help to restore muscles to their resting length after the continual contraction involved in running, help to maintain range of motion in the joints and prevent tightness and imbalances between muscle groups.

Six more reasons to stretch
● A flexible joint uses less energy to work through its full range of motion, so good flexibility will enable you to run more efficiently.
● Increased supply of blood and nutrients to joint structures helps keep them healthy and mobile.
● Stretching improves neuromuscular coordination (the nerve impulses that travel from the body to the brain and back).

When not to do it
Never stretch cold muscles. This doesn't just mean physically cold, but any time when muscles are dormant, lying at rest. In other words, when you've just got up in the morning or from a long spell at your desk. It's essential to raise your muscle temperature prior to stretching. You can do this with heat rather than an active warm-up if necessary (when, for example, you are injured) by using heat packs or a warm bath.

How to stretch effectively

There are four important points to consider in a successful stretch:

● Are you doing the stretch properly? Many people simply mimic another runner's stretch without really knowing what muscle group they're stretching or how to get the technique and position right. The stretch sequence on pages 36–38 will help you avoid this pitfall. You should stretch to the point at which you feel tension and a slight pulling sensation in the muscle but not pain. Hold this position until the stretch reflex occurs and the force on the muscle decreases. Then increase the stretch if you can and continue to hold.

● Are you holding it for long enough? The latest research from the American College of Sports Medicine recommends holding stretches for 20–30 seconds and repeating each one two to four times. But we are all different. The journal *Physician and Sports Medicine* found that, while the standard 20–30-second protocol worked for most people and most muscle groups, some people need to stretch for longer, or do more repetitions of each stretch. For example, the hamstring muscles showed decreased stiffness only after five repeated stretches, while the hip abductor range of motion didn't increase further after a 15-second stretch compared to a 2-minute one.

● Are you doing it regularly enough? While in an ideal world we would stretch every day, at least stretch on every running or other workout day.

● Are you stretching the muscles you need to? Many runners overlook a number of important muscles in their stretching regimen, such as the deep calves and adductors.

The runner's stretch

The sequence that starts on the next page is based on static stretching (where you assume a position and hold it for a given period). It targets all the main muscle groups that are relevant to runners, but you may want to add other stretches to the sequence (such as any a physical therapist has prescribed) that are personal to your own body and any injuries or limitations you have.

Perform the stretches in the order shown, beginning with the back-mobilizing exercises on pages 122–123. These ensure that the spinal structures are free and not causing any tightness in the legs.

Do each of the following stretches two to four times, paying more attention to your tighter areas, and holding each stretch for 30 seconds. Gradually increase the stretch as comfort and resistance allow. Remember to stretch both sides of the body where necessary.

PROPRIOCEPTIVE NEUROMUSCULAR FACILITATION (PNF)

This is a specific type of stretching that "tricks" the propriopceptive organs to allow a stretch to be taken further. For example, you might take your hamstring into a stretch and then get a partner to hold the leg in the stretched position while you push against them (as if trying to get out of the stretch). You do this for 10 seconds and then relax, and your partner gently pushes your leg further into a stretch. PNF stretching can produce impressive results but it causes more post-stretch soreness and is much less convenient than static stretching, especially if you don't have a willing partner. A review study in *Physician and Sports Medicine* looked at more than 60 studies on stretching and concluded that a static stretch was effective for most people.

1 Gluteals (bottom)

Starting position: Lie on your back on the floor.

Exercise: Cross your right foot over the left knee, keeping the right knee out to the side, and take hold of the left leg behind the thigh. Draw the leg toward you until you feel a stretch in the right hip and gluteal area. Swap sides.

2 Adductors (inner thighs)

Starting position: Sit on the floor.

Exercise: Bend the knees and let the legs fall out, drawing the soles of the feet together. Using your elbows, gently push down on the inside of the knees.

Now take the legs astride and straighten them, keeping the head up and the chest forward.

3 Hamstrings (back of thighs)

Starting position: Sit on the floor with your left leg out straight and the right leg bent with the foot against the left leg.

Exercise: Keeping the head up and chest forward, lean over the left leg, hinging from the hip, rather than curving your lower back. Take hold of the part of the leg you can reach, or loop a towel over the foot, and hold the stretch. Gradually aim to reach further down the leg.

4 Hip flexors (front of hips)

Starting position: Lunge forward, placing your left foot on the floor in front and your right leg out behind, knee resting on the floor.

Exercise: Keeping the pelvis in a neutral position (it's easiest to do this by gently tightening the tummy muscles), slowly lean forward. You should feel a stretch on the front of the hip. Don't let the back arch – keep up tall. This is a basic hip flexor stretch – for a more advanced option, see the Thomas stretch on page 39.

5 Quadriceps (front of thighs)

Starting position: Stand upright. Bend one knee behind you and take hold of the foot with the same hand.

Exercise: Now bring the foot to the bottom, taking care not to arch the back, tip the pelvis forward or bend forward with the torso. If you don't feel a stretch, pull the knee backward.

If you find it hard to keep your spine and pelvis neutral, try this alternative. Start in the hip flexor stretch position (see page 37), but place your back knee on a cushion. Take hold of the foot, pull up tall in the torso and you should feel a stretch along the front of the thigh.

6 Calf stretch (back of lower leg)

This stretch has three stages, because there are three layers of calf muscle. The deep layer is especially important to runners, as it can cause shin pain when too tight.

Starting position: Stand facing a wall in a split stance (you will be stretching the back leg) with the front leg bent and back leg straight.

Exercise: Lean into the wall, keeping your pelvis beneath you and back heel on the ground **(a)**. Make sure your feet are pointing directly forward and not splaying out to the side. You should feel the stretch on the lower part of the back leg – if you don't, move the back leg further away from the wall. Next, simply bend the back knee so you feel the stretch deeper in the calf muscle rather than behind the knee **(b)**. Finally, to stretch the deep layer, bring the toes of the back foot up against the heel of the front foot **(c)**. Keep the knees bent.

a b c

7 Thomas stretch

This is a more advanced version of the hip flexor stretch, which also stretches the quadriceps and ITB (iliotibial band). You'll need a surface about mid-thigh height. The kitchen table is normally a good bet!

Starting position: Stand with your buttocks resting against a table or use the steeplechase pit at your local track.

Exercise: Pull one knee to your chest and slowly lie back onto the table, keeping the knee pulled into your chest. If you take a look at the stretching leg, it should be in line with, or below, the level of the table. If it is higher than that, this indicates tightness in your hip flexors. If, when you bend the leg, the thigh rises up, this indicates tightness in the quads, specifically the rectus femoris.

Allow the stretching leg to hang off the table, gently pressing the knee downward without letting the back arch. If possible, get someone to push down gently on the top of the knee.

If you have a helper, you can also try a PNF stretch technique (see box on page 35) called contract and relax, where you push your thigh up against their hand for five seconds and then relax, which should enable you to increase the stretch.

To stretch the quadriceps, the heel needs to go back toward the buttock. Get your helper to hold your knee in place and manually bring your heel backward. Remember, this stretch should not cause pain – just tolerable discomfort.

Touching a nerve

You may not give them much thought, but your nerves play a big role in your movements, your posture and your perception of pain, and they deserve a little attention. Just like muscles, nerves can get sore or inflamed and lose their natural range and mobility – and just as with muscles, poor biomechanics, injuries and imbalances can cause problems. Because of the repetitive nature of running, it is possible to get micro trauma and inflammation anywhere along the line of the nerve, especially if it is already tight in the spine. While we don't stretch nerves in the same way as we stretch muscles, it is possible to mobilize them. To mobilize a nerve, we put it on tension and then move one structure in and out of the tense position, as if we were "flossing" the nerve. The nerve is never held in tension, as this can damage the blood vessels supplying it.

The two most important nerves for runners are the sciatic nerve and the femoral nerve, both of which emerge from the vertebrae of the lower back. The sciatic nerve comes from the junction between the lumbar and sacral vertebrae, passing under – or sometimes through – the piriformis muscle in the glutes, through the hamstrings and around the head of the fibula down to the feet. On its journey through the body, the nerve has to run the gauntlet of a lot of potential problems. First, it has to emerge from the spine without any impingement from a bulging disc or a tight facet joint. Then it has to pass through various muscle fascia interfaces and even around corners, where it can become snagged. A common problem is "tethering" – when a nerve literally becomes stuck to surrounding structures as a result of bleeding and inflammation around an injured muscle. Nerve mobilizations can help to prevent this.

Sciatic nerve mobilizations

There are three mobilizations for the sciatic nerve that focus on different areas of the body.

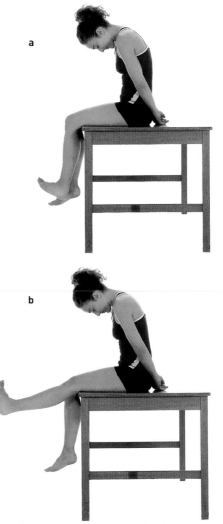

a

b

The slump

Purpose: This exercise is good for hamstring and gluteal tension.

Starting position: Sit on a chair (or table, if possible) and bend the head and trunk so you are effectively slumped in the chair **(a)**.

Exercise: To mobilize the nerve, flex the foot and straighten the knee, then swing the leg up and down **(b)**. Don't hold the position with the leg out straight. Do three sets of 10.

Long sitting

Purpose: This exercise is helpful for any tension behind the knee.

Starting position: Sit on the floor with the legs out straight **(a)**.

Exercise: Bend the head and trunk forward and pull the toes of one foot toward you. Relax the leg and bounce the knee up and down, from straight through about 30 degrees **(b)**. Do three sets of 10.

a

b

Straight-leg raise

Purpose: Eases calf and Achilles tightness.

Starting position: Lie on your back on the floor with one leg in the air. If you need some support, put the leg against a doorframe with the relaxed leg through the door.

Exercise: Looping a towel or belt around the raised foot, flex and release the foot, keeping the leg straight. Do three sets of 10.

Femoral nerve mobilization

The femoral nerve originates from the higher lumbar vertebrae and supplies the front of the thigh. It may need to be mobilized if there is tightness in the hip flexors or quadriceps. If you have a nondescript knee pain, it's also worth trying this to ease any tightness.

Adapted Thomas stretch

Starting position: Adopt the Thomas stretch position, as described on page 39.

Exercise: Now lift the head – chin to chest – and swing the free leg rhythmically underneath heel to buttock and back. Do three sets of 10.

If you don't have a suitable surface for the Thomas stretch position, adopt a kneeling position with one leg in front, foot on the floor. Take hold of the foot of the bent leg behind, bend the head and trunk forward and lift the head up and down. Do three sets of 10.

chapter 4

down to earth

the importance of what's on your feet and under them

The shoes you run in are the most important piece of equipment you own. A recent report from California State University shows that impact forces during running vary from between one and a half and five times your body weight – so you need some protection, and that protection should be designed specifically to meet the demands of running.

Along with cushioning and shock absorption, running shoes offer varying degrees of support and stability, as well as "motion control" features to influence the biomechanics of your feet. But how can you tell what type of trainer you need?

Determining your footwear needs

Your individual footwear needs depend on your foot type and how you run. Broadly speaking, there are three types of runners: the neutral runner, the overpronator and the oversupinator. It is believed that as many as 70 percent of runners are overpronators, and much of the technology that goes into shoes is designed to address this problem. Here are some easy ways to start to get a picture of which category you fit into.

The wet footprint test
1 Toe prints plus heel but little in between indicate high arches, which are associated with excessive supination, or underpronation.

2 Entire or almost all of foot shows: low or flat arches, often associated with overpronation.

3 Toes and forefoot plus heel, joined by a broad band: normal or "neutral" footstrike.

Wet footprint test

Dunk your feet in water and then walk across a flat, even surface, such as concrete, hard sand or a sheet of cardboard. Compare what you see to the images opposite. This test is by no means a replacement for professional gait analysis, but it can provide clues as to how your foot strikes the ground.

Look at your feet

Look at the medial side of your feet (toward the big toe) while standing. Is there no discernible arch? If you bend your knees, do the feet roll in, with the knees following? These are indications of overpronation.

If the feet have high arches that don't flatten or roll in at all when you bend your knees, you are more likely to be an excessive supinator.

If you are somewhere in between – if you can see an arch, which has a bit of give when you bend (and the knees don't drift in) – your feet are fairly neutral.

The Adidas footscan

The Adidas footscan device uses digital imaging to create a "picture" of your foot, showing where most of the pressure is exerted during normal standing and when your foot lands during running. You stand, and then run, on the pressure-sensitive pad, which has over 8000 sensors built into it, while the footscan records your foot's movements at a rate of 500 frames per second. Specialist software then interprets this data to provide a graphic representation of your foot strike pattern, which can be used to determine the best type of shoe for your needs. Many specialist running shops offer this as a free service.

Examine old shoes

Your old running shoes can provide valuable clues as to what type of runner you are. The normal place to see signs of wear on the shoe is the outside of the heel and over the ball of the foot. If the medial side

of the front is worn, this indicates that you may be an overpronator. If the wear remains on the outside of the shoe, you may be an oversupinator.

Place your running shoe on a flat surface and examine the heel cup from behind. Does it look as if it has been forced down toward the medial side of the shoe? This indicates that you have been collapsing in on this side of the shoe because of overpronation – and that the shoe isn't doing a good enough job of supporting the foot.

Finally, do the twist test (see photo above). Take hold of the shoe at each end and twist it. It should feel nice and firm. An old shoe, or one that hasn't given proper support, will twist easily.

Ask the experts

Above all, ask the experts for some advice. You should be able to get help at most specialist running shops. Expect to have your feet examined (they may watch you walk or run) and to be asked lots of questions about your running experience and ability, your mileage, what surfaces you run on, your weight and any injury problems. Podiatrists and physical therapists with special knowledge of sport and running are also a useful source of information. You may want to consider having gait analysis, which you can read more about on page 21.

Running shoe anatomy

Now that you know a little more about your needs, let's look at the shoes themselves. There are three principal types: stability shoes, cushioned shoes and motion control shoes. Generally speaking, an oversupinator needs to look for more cushioning, an overpronator needs motion control and features, and a neutral runner needs a mix of control and cushioning – a stability shoe.

Shoes are built around a last, which is a foot-shaped mold. This determines the shape of the shoe and some of its qualities. A last can be curved, straight or semicurved. On a straight-lasted shoe, a line drawn lengthways, starting at the midpoint of the heel and passing along the sole to the toes, would hit the point where the second toe lies. On a curved or semicurved last, that line passes closer to the little toe. The straighter the last, the more support given to the medial side of the foot, which means these shoes are better for the overpronator. However, there has been a recent move by shoe manufacturers to stop "overcontrolling" the foot, and some anti-pronation shoes are now built on a semicurved last, with other technological devices used to address and mitigate the problem.

Most of the technology in a running shoe is housed in its midsole, the bit that sits between the inner sole and the outsole. Here the trend has been toward producing thinner midsoles to enhance the sensation for the runner and make running more "natural."

A motion control shoe has a firmer midsole, often with a medial post inserted on the medial side of the midsole near the back. This is made from a firmer-density foam, sometimes with a plastic insert, to prevent the foot rolling inward. A midfoot "shank" is used to add stability – this is a plastic insert built into the midsole around the arch area. A firmer heel counter is also used in a motion control shoe to support the rear part of the foot.

Cushioned shoes are for oversupinators whose rigid, high-arched foot doesn't give them any shock absorbency. These shoes need more cushioning to compensate for the lack of shock absorption and are usually built on a curved or semicurved last to encourage some pronation and movement. Cushioned shoes also have a softer midsole and no additional medial support.

The stability shoe is the happy medium, providing a blend of cushioning, medial support and stability. The medial support may come from a dual-density midsole, which is firmer where more support is needed, but isn't as extreme as a medial post. This shoe is usually built on a semicurved last.

Heel counter or cup This provides a snug fit around the heel to control the rearfoot. Memory foam is being used in some brands to allow personal fit and maximum contouring around the heel.

Insole This is normally an extra layer inside for comfort and can have features that keep the feet cool and fresh, usually antibacterial.

Midsole The most important part of the shoe, this is made from ethylene and vinyl acetate (EVA), which is lightweight and a good shock absorber. Depending on the density, the EVA allows for greater cushioning or support. Some shoes offer extra shock absorption with substances such as gel or air: this can either be focused in the rear foot or distributed across the whole length of the shoe.

Upper This is the bit that encases the foot and holds the lacing case, with reinforcement in various places to ensure a snug fit. It is usually made from a tight-weave mesh that adds strength and durability, but allows the foot to breathe.

Reflective strip Normally found on the back of the shoe, this helps with night visibility.

Outsole This is the rubber outer layer that sits under the shoe. It can be either blown rubber (lightweight, very cushioned but not durable) or carbon runner (harder, more solid and heavy, but more durable) or a combination of both.

Laces These hold the shoe snug to the foot.

Flex grooves These allow the forefoot to flex and need to be strategically placed to allow for natural flexing of the forefoot.

Ten-point guide to buying a pair of running shoes

1 Make sure you have plenty of time, and don't rush. Research from the Medical College of Wisconsin shows that the wrong shoes may play a role in the development of stress fractures.

2 Go to a specialist running shop where the staff members are experienced in fitting running shoes. It helps if they are runners, too. A *Which?* study in 2000 found that the advice given at most chain sports stores on trainers was well below par.

3 Go later on in the day when your feet are slightly larger to ensure you get a good fit.

4 Take your old shoes with you so the staff can look at wear patterns.

5 Wear appropriate clothing so you can try the shoes out properly. A lot of shops now have treadmills to look at how you run and for you to test the shoes on.

6 Take your running socks with you. If you wear orthotics, take them along too.

7 Make sure the shoes are comfortable in the shop. If they are not, they won't be for running.

8 Don't be swayed by appearances or brands. Try on several makes and models.

9 Don't go by what your friend wears as they may run completely differently from you.

10 Be prepared to invest. Shoes will last 300–500 miles, so it is worth spending more to get a decent pair, rather than opting for the bargain bin!

How should shoes fit?

The shoe should feel comfortable as soon as you put it on. There should be enough room in the toebox for you to wiggle the toes around, and you should be able to fit your index finger between the longest toe – usually the big toe – and the end of the shoe. Some shoes are more rounded at the ends, while others taper off toward the little toe, so make sure the lateral side of the toebox doesn't rub your toes. There also needs to be sufficient width to accommodate the foot comfortably. Women often have a narrower heel but broader forefoot than men, and female-specific shoes take this into account. But if any shoe feels too tight across the foot, try a different brand, as they each have a slightly different fit. The heel should be firm but not pinching, and you don't want your heel to slip up and down inside the shoe. Make sure the heel tab at the top of the heel cup does not dig into your Achilles tendon. Walk around in the shoes and, if possible, try to run in them.

Lacing techniques

Make sure you carefully lace your shoe before running. It sounds obvious, but if you are in a hurry, or not really concentrating, it's easy just to shove on your shoes and lace them any old way. But too tight, and the shoe can make parts of the top of your foot sore and squeeze your metatarsals too tightly. Too loose, and the shoe may allow your foot to move excessively, reducing stability and increasing the likelihood of blisters.

How you lace your shoes can also make a big difference on the fit. If you need a more secure fit, loop-lock the last hole, which just means you pull the lace back through the next hole to form a loop, and then pull the opposite loose end through the loop (see opposite, left). As you pull the laces tight, you'll feel it secure the heel in place. If the shoe feels too

tight, you can slide the lace along a few of the bottom eyelets on one side without crisscrossing over to allow a bit more give (see above, right).

Running shoes and injury

If you get injured, ask yourself the following questions about your shoes:

1 Have I just changed my shoes? If so, go back to the old model and see if that helps.
2 Are the shoes worn out?
3 Are they the correct shoes for my foot type?
4 Is the heel tab pinching my Achilles?
5 Has the midsole collapsed?
6 Has the air pocket in the shoe punctured?

Orthotics
If you've taken advice on the right shoes but still don't seem to be able to rid yourself of problems, it may be worth considering orthotics. These are custom-built footbeds that help to put the foot in the correct position so that it can work naturally. They are most commonly used to correct overpronation. You can either get orthotics made to fit by a podiatrist (see Resources), or go for cheaper, off-the-shelf versions, which can normally be ordered by your physical therapist. These may work just fine and are normally a good test to see if you need proper orthotics, which can be very expensive.

TIME FOR A NEW PAIR?

A failsafe guide for whether you need a new pair of shoes is to look at the sole. If it's worn out, trash them! The sole lasts much longer than the shock absorbency of the midsole.

Shoes should last approximately six months or 300–500 miles worth of running. To make them last as long as possible, wear your running shoes only for running, never put them in the washing machine, and always look after them. Don't take them on and off with the laces done up. Do rinse them after muddy runs, as dampness can rot the stitching. And don't dry them on the radiator: take out the insoles and let them dry naturally, away from direct heat.

Specialist shoes

Racing shoes

If you are an experienced runner, then you may want to try either a performance shoe or a racing flat. These are a lot lighter and allow faster work to be performed. Be warned, though, that these shoes are fairly stripped of the support and cushioning features of regular training shoes and should be worn sparingly for races and speed work.

Spikes

Spikes are shoes with a forefoot spike plate to allow extra grip. These are suitable for cross-country and track work. Spikes have a very different feel from trainers because the foot sits a lot closer to the ground, giving a negative heel (a heel that is lower than the rest of the foot). This can overload the calf, as it has to work more eccentrically (contracting while lengthening), and can cause calf and Achilles problems. These typically occur at the start of the track season when spikes are first worn. Make sure you buy a pair suitable for middle-distance running or cross-country, as they will have more support and a slightly better heel than spikes designed for sprinting.

Trail shoes

Trail or off-road shoes have better grip on the outsole, usually provided by "lugs" or other knobbly protrusions. They will normally have a more robust upper – sometimes made from a water-resistant or waterproof fabric – and a reinforced toebox to protect your toes from rough ground.

> SARAH'S CASEBOOK
>
> The shoe I run in, and find most suitable for overpronators who need some motion control, is the Asics Gel Kayano.

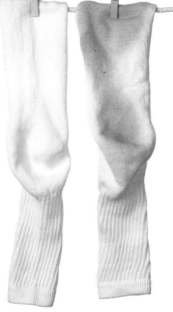

Running socks

Now that you've spent so much time and effort on getting the right shoes, don't ruin it all by buying cheap, poor-quality socks! Ill-fitting or inappropriate fabric socks can cause infections, blisters and black toenails and can even contribute to the wearing away of the "fat pads" that cushion the feet. The right socks (and, as with shoes, that means socks designed specifically for running) can offer extra protection, reduce friction, keep feet cool, wick away sweat and prevent foot slippage (which can cause blisters). Studies show that cotton socks are not a good idea, as they retain three times the moisture of acrylic ones and fourteen times the moisture of technical fabrics like Coolmax and Dri-fit.

The other problem with cotton is that, when wet, it becomes shapeless, leading to bunching and wrinkling, and after a few washes it can become hard and abrasive. Technical fabrics are definitely the way to go – some socks even have special features like antibacterial fibers and strategic cushioning. See Resources (page 181) for some suggested manufacturers. If you are plagued with blisters, it's worth trying double-layer socks in which the outer layer moves with the shoe while the inner layer stays with the foot, thus eliminating friction on the skin.

Under your feet

Even if you have the most supportive, protective shoes that money can buy, you still need to think about what is underfoot and aim to do at least some of your training on more forgiving surfaces than concrete. While reducing the impact on your joints is the primary reason for doing this, varying your surfaces also challenges your musculoskeletal, neuromuscular and cardiovascular systems in different ways.

Research in the *British Journal of Sports Medicine* found that heart rate varied significantly when the same runners ran on different surfaces and was more variable off-road than on-road. (There was a 44 bpm variation during an off-road run, compared to just 10 beats on-road.) It also appears that there are individual differences in response to different surfaces, probably as a result of previous experience of running on those surfaces.

On the road

For many of us, road running is a necessity at least some of the time because of the lack of alternatives. If you race on roads, it's important that you do train on them anyway. We call it "road running," but usually we're running on the sidewalk. A pedantic point, you might think, but many sidewalks are made of concrete, while roads are generally made from asphalt, which has slightly more "give." If it's safe to do so, run on the road rather than on sidewalks when you have the choice. The grass edge of the road is even better. But beware of running on the edge of a steeply slanted road, as the tilted surface can contribute to injury problems, particularly iliotibial band friction syndrome (see page 141).

Trail mix

Running off-road is undoubtedly more demanding than running on sidewalks – a fact easily demonstrated by running on the rough terrain next to a concrete path and feeling how you decelerate. What makes it more challenging is also what makes it less punishing on your joints: a softer, more yielding surface. The changing terrain and gradient also create more work for the lower legs, which have to stabilize you on the uneven surface, which has what's known as a high "damping ratio" (meaning it doesn't "give" you much back). One study found that the energy cost of running through a forest was 26 percent greater than running at the same pace on a road, which the researchers put down to changes in stride biomechanics that demanded more oxygen. Other research found that step length and speed decreased and knee lift increased on rougher terrain (they compared running on a footpath to running on short grass and long grass).

You'll probably run more slowly off-road, but don't worry too much about that because as far as your heart and lungs are concerned, it's just as challenging as faster paces on-road – and you're improving your coordination and ability to stabilize all the while.

What's more, the variety provided by an uneven surface works different muscles and slightly breaks the overuse pattern that can cause injuries. It's worth doing at least one or two runs a week on trail, grass or mixed rough terrain to give your joints a break and reap these benefits. Think about maintaining the same effort level as on-road, rather than the same speed, to avoid tiring yourself out.

Get on track

An athletics track offers one of the most joint-friendly surfaces imaginable, with a huge amount of elastic return. Research in the *Journal of Applied Physiology* shows that increased energy rebound from compliant surfaces, such as a synthetic track, reduces metabolic cost, so you get more "bang for your buck."

However, this isn't necessarily tendon-friendly. The high elastic return means the Achilles tendon has to store and pay out much more energy, thereby working harder and increasing the risk of problems. Be aware, too, that you always run in the same direction on a track, which can cause imbalances between the left and right sides, so don't do too much of your training there. Also, don't wear spikes unless you are doing real speed work – such as 200 m reps or less – because the lack of heel raise makes them much less protective than normal trainers. Racing flats put less stress on the Achilles than spikes.

If you don't currently use a track, here are five good reasons to give it a go:

- It's easily measurable.
- You are never more than 400 m away from a drink, toilet or your clothing.
- It's safe.
- It's flat and even.
- It's kinder to your joints.

Not just run-of-the-mill
A treadmill is another less impactful alternative to running on concrete, but don't get too addicted: you may feel as if you are running in the same way as you would outdoors, but the biomechanics are slightly different because you are staying on the spot rather than moving forward. This often results in a lower leg lift and stiffer stride, in order to control the foot being dragged backward and in pulling the lower leg forward. A recent study in the *International Journal of Sports Medicine* found that stride length was reduced while stride frequency was increased in treadmill running. The "swing" of the leg was lower, the foot flatter at contact point, and contact time with the ground shorter. In other research, on elite distance runners, it was found that a higher maximum running speed was achieved on a track compared to on a treadmill.

So that's the bad news. But what's the good news? Well, of course, access to a treadmill means that you

can run safely at any time, and avoid inclement weather. The treadmill also offers a uniquely controllable environment. You can monitor and control your speed and incline precisely – particularly useful for interval training or speed sessions. It can also be a good option for those returning from – or prone to – injury, because the "give" of the surface reduces impact.

Treadmill tips
- Don't look down at the controls or at your feet – this can throw your posture out of alignment.
- Do use the treadmill for shorter sessions and not long runs to avoid altering your stride mechanics.
- Set the gradient to 2 percent. Research from Brighton University found that this more closely mimicked outdoor running than having it flat, as you don't have to cope with wind resistance or erratic terrain indoors.
- Allow yourself a good warm-up. Research from La Trobe University in Australia suggests that it takes around six minutes to become familiarized with a treadmill. In the study, runners made adjustments to their stride, cadence and postural alignment before settling into a pattern after this period.

balancing act

the art and science of training

Even with a strong core, top-of-the-range shoes and technique to rival Gebrselassie's, bad training habits could still send the whole thing spinning. Such as? Not taking sufficient rest. Running all your sessions at 90 percent effort. Bingeing on running and then not exercising for weeks. Many experts believe that running injuries are predominantly caused not by biomechanical problems but by training errors. The good news is that means they are easily remedied. How? By learning how to train smarter.

Smart training is all about getting the most you can out of your training. It's about pushing yourself, but stopping before you reach the point of injury. It's about continuously progressing, but only at a rate that your body can cope with. Most of all, it's about balance. A balance between rest and activity; between fast, hard sessions and slow, easy ones; between running and other activities.

Take Dan. He's a decent runner, attempting the marathon distance for the first time. As soon as he found out he had an entry, he upped his mileage from 30 miles a week to 50 by running six days a week instead of four (running for 2.5 hours on Sunday mornings). Of course, Dan's intentions are good. He knows that he is going to have to get used to running for prolonged periods and that he needs to increase his usual mileage in order to prepare for the marathon – but his approach is all wrong. Let's look in detail at the key ingredients of a good training program to see what's lacking.

Why do we train?

Training is the method we use to make the body adapt so that it can do the things we want it to. In essence, it means doing something more challenging than what we are accustomed to. The body is "overloaded" with a task (for example, a run longer or faster than it is used to) that it completes. It then makes the necessary adaptations in order to be able to cope more easily with that challenge next time around. "Progressive overload" is the scientific term for this, and going back to our friend Dan, it's the "progressive" element that's been left out of his training. He's just leapt from doing 30 miles to 50 in a week, while experts recommend adding no more than 10 percent to your mileage on a weekly basis, with the occasional week of no increase at all. Having been on a weekly 30-mile diet, he could have safely increased his mileage to 33, then 36–37 the week after. At that rate of progression, it would take 5–6 weeks to reach the 50-mile total that he leapt to in one fell swoop, markedly increasing his risk of injury – not to mention extreme fatigue.

What changes?
So what's actually happening in the body to make it more able to cope with these new challenges next time around? Changes occur

DON'T RUN BEFORE YOU CAN WALK

If you are new to running, it is essential to get the rate of progression right. Too fast and you risk pain, injury, disillusionment and, worst of all, giving up altogether. (Too slow, mind you, and you risk not progressing at all – but we'll come back to that!) This means progressing from walking to mixing bouts of walking and running and then to running only.

Once you've got to the point at which you can run continuously for, say, 20 minutes, focus on building your endurance by increasing the time to 30, 40 and 50 minutes. Only once you can do this comfortably should you add in tougher stuff like speed work and intervals.

Now, this doesn't mean suddenly making all of your runs faster and harder. The risk of injury increases markedly when you are running at a pace beyond your comfort zone. Fast sessions shouldn't make up more than 10 percent of your total mileage/training – having a mix of different-paced runs is far more valuable. The best thing is to make one of your weekly runs a shorter, faster session, while increasing the duration (but not the speed) of another one. So instead of having, say, four runs all at the same pace and distance, you have two steady runs: a shorter, faster one and a longer, slower one. Now it's shaping up to be a training program and not just a weekly routine of running.

throughout the body as a result of regular running. For example, the tendons and ligaments become more robust, the muscles become stronger and more able to withstand long periods of constant contraction. The lungs become more efficient at taking in air and the left ventricle of the heart, the one that pumps oxygenated blood around the body, strengthens so that it can pump out more blood with every beat. The body also becomes more efficient at

storing precious glycogen (the body's storage form of carbohydrate) and at utilizing fat as a fuel. Studies show increases of up to 40 percent in glycogen storage in trained runners, while the body's capacity to use fat as an energy source (thereby "sparing" glycogen) can increase by as much as 30 percent. But all these changes don't take place while you are running; they happen when you are resting.

Give it a rest

Rest is perhaps one of the most overlooked components of a training program. If you imagine progressive overload as a staircase, with your goal perching at the top, each time you add a new level of challenge, your body needs to rest and recover in order to make the necessary adaptations. If you don't allow this vital recovery time, you won't make it up to the next step. Poor old Dan, training pretty hard six days a week, hasn't factored in the importance of rest and isn't likely to be getting the maximum benefits from his running. Then again, Dan's buddy Phil, who is also taking on the marathon for the first time, won't be getting the maximum benefit from his training either, because he has spent more time resting than he has training! It's been shown that two weeks of complete inactivity in well-trained runners results in a 9 percent drop in performance. The best way to factor in rest is to intersperse hard training sessions with rest days, rather than training hard until you're so exhausted that you are forced to take a rest day. Want another good reason to avoid running when you are fatigued? Research from the University of Nevada found that shock attenuation was 12 percent lower and oxygen consumption 16 percent greater when runners were made to run on a treadmill after a maximal-effort exercise test than when they ran "fresh."

Exactly how much rest to take is an individual thing. Some people can't bear a day or two without exercise, while others are happy training three days a week. When you're planning your program, remember that, unlike

SARAH'S CASEBOOK

After a hard session, try some self-massage (if you can't find a willing volunteer!). I use a product containing arnica to settle any inflammation, applying it to the main muscle groups – the hamstrings, quads and calves – and working up toward the heart. This helps disperse all the waste products of training and breaks down any small adhesions and knots.

the elite athletes, you also have to balance training with work, family, friends, hobbies, chores and a social life, so you need to be realistic about how much you can fit in without ending up frazzled.

Also bear in mind that rest and recovery don't necessarily mean doing nothing. In fact, while strategies to enhance recovery are part of every elite athlete's regimen, they are often woefully overlooked by recreational runners of all standards.

Make a full recovery

Paula Radcliffe famously swears by a post-run ice bath, but what does the evidence say? Most of the research on this has been done by a researcher in Australia named Angela Calder, who, thankfully, advises the use of contrast bathing – alternating hot and cold – as preferable to sitting still in an ice bath. Ideally this should be done within the hour after your session, and the easiest way to put it into practice is to alternate the temperature of a shower from hot to cold. Try 30 seconds of each, three times. If there is no hot shower, use cold interspersed by rubbing with a towel. Brrrr!

Perhaps more appealing is the idea of a massage. While there is scant evidence on sports massage aiding recovery, that doesn't stop the majority of elite athletes relying on it – and there is plenty of anecdotal evidence to suggest that it does assist recovery. Proponents of sports massage claim that it increases blood flow to damaged tissues, helping their recovery, stretches and realigns muscle fibers and reduces the likelihood of muscle tension and spasm. Some research contests this. For example, a study in the *Journal of Athletic Training* in 2005 found no beneficial effect on post-exercise muscle soreness after massage. But then again, the subjects received only a five-minute treatment! It's worth bearing in mind that regular sports massage gives the practitioner an opportunity to spot any problem areas that, if unobserved and untreated, could turn into injuries later on. In a report published in the *British Journal of Sports Medicine*, no scientific evidence was found to support the idea that sports massage improves physio-logical recovery after exercise, but the researchers conceded that the subjects' enhanced perception of recovery lent some support to the use of massage as a recovery practice. Other research shows raised endorphin levels post-massage, which may explain its feel-good effect.

A final consideration, if you want to function normally – not to mention run well – the day after a hard session, is replenishing your body's energy supply. Carbohydrate and fluids come at the top of the list, while a little protein helps muscle recovery and regeneration. You need to put your refueling strategy into action as soon as possible after your run, as studies show that carbohydrate taken in within the first one to two hours is more readily converted into glycogen, the fuel stored in your muscles and liver. If you can't tolerate food straight away, opt for an isotonic sports drink (which replaces both lost salts and fluids) or a recovery drink with added protein. Always carry fresh fruit, too, to boost antioxidant and vitamin intake. You can read more about nutrition and hydration in chapter 9.

Be consistent

Whether it's three or six days a week that you decide on for your running regimen, make it consistent. The body doesn't like sporadic training because it doesn't know whether or not it needs to adapt to a new level of challenge. One minute it does, and then it gets a week off and allows those adaptations to slide – only to find it is called upon to produce them again the following week. Leaving too long between training sessions will allow the window of opportunity to close. So while Dan's body is close to breakdown point, Phil's is saying, "Ah, doesn't look like we'll be doing that session again, so I won't bother to make the adaptations." When this happens, the principle of "reversibility" comes into play, meaning that instead of improving and moving up a step on the staircase, you stay on the same stair, or even backslide a step or two.

As you can see, even with the right level of progressive overload and the right amount of rest, without consistency it all falls apart. The time when elite athletes – already so close to their maximum ability – improve is when they can train consistently without being bugged by injury or illness, and the same goes for you (even though it may be reasons other than illness or injury that hamper your consistency!). That doesn't mean you can never ever skip a training day; it simply means that you should aim to train regularly when there isn't a good reason not to.

As well as being consistent in a broad sense (making sure you train regularly), it's also important to be consistent with the sessions themselves. For example, a random hill or drill session will have little benefit. You need to repeat it regularly and make progress for it to be valuable. That's why you need a game plan for your training and why structure is so important.

What kind of training?

In order to structure your training successfully, you need to know what to build with – that is, what the ingredients should be. This depends partly on your personal running goals – training just for general fitness is very different from training for a half marathon or marathon, for instance. But if you want to make progress as opposed to getting stuck on that stair, there are some key elements you need to consider.

Mix it up

The first of these is variety, in terms of the type of sessions you do. Even for a marathon, it isn't all about quantity but about quality. That's why our friend Dan, even if he makes it to the starting line, isn't likely to perform as well as he could have done in that marathon. He – and you – should mix hard and easy sessions, long and short ones, steady and fast, flat and hilly, off-road and on-road.

As you can see, there are lots and lots of options as far as types of run are concerned, and yet many of us simply repeat the same old sessions, at the same pace, time after time, and then wonder why we aren't improving!

The specificity principle

Before we look at some of the most important sessions and the benefits they offer, a word about specificity. Another of the key principles of sports training, this means that you should practice the activity you want to get better at, in order to get better at it. In other words, if you want to run a marathon, don't enroll in a ballet course. If you want to swim the English Channel, don't go running three times a week. While there is plenty of evidence that specificity is important and a valid principle to abide by, it doesn't mean that to become better at, say, running steady for a prolonged period, you should only ever run steady for a long period. It's important to include a reasonable amount of that in your program, but you'll benefit more by balancing those steady runs with some different types of training. Find out why in the next three chapters.

chapter 6

smart sessions

why and how to vary your runs

The key variables you have to play with, in terms of varying your running sessions, are pace and time – or, to put it another way, intensity and distance. If you train smart, as you increase one, you decrease the other, so that you are trying to run for longer or run harder – not both at the same time, which could put you at risk of extreme fatigue and possible injury.

A common mistake runners make is to manipulate too many variables at once. If you are increasing speed, don't increase length of time too. If you are increasing the number of times you run a week, don't also try to run harder. Otherwise your overload isn't progressive, it's aggressive.

The benefits of longer runs

Running at a steady, comfortable pace for a prolonged period is fantastic for priming the heart, circulatory system and lungs. It improves your muscular endurance, increases the amount of oxygen your hardworking leg muscles can squeeze out of the blood, enhances your use of fat as a fuel, burns calories and helps you develop stronger, more resilient connective tissues. These runs should be your staple diet. (Dan at least got that bit right.)

If you race, or are planning to race, distances of 10K or more (and especially if you are aiming for a half or full marathon), a "long" run is an essential element of your schedule. In essence, it's a longer version of a steady run, generally taken at a comfortable pace, although as you progress it's worth doing a proportion of your long runs at race pace. One study found that the most important factor in determining successful completion of a marathon was the length of the competitor's longest training run. This was even more important than total weekly mileage or the number of marathons already run. But even if you don't intend to go for the magical 26.2 miles, you can benefit physically and psychologically from a regular long run. How long? Again that depends on your personal goals, time, inclination and fitness. Start by increasing your current maximum running time or distance by 10 percent. That's your starting point. Increase the length of this run by 10 percent each time you do it (which should be at least every two weeks in order to benefit). If you do a long run weekly, allow a week off every four to five weeks, and try to do some of your long runs off-road to reduce the overall impact on your joints.

The benefits of running harder

You probably don't need much persuasion to include steady runs in your schedule, as these are the ones most of us, like Dan, instinctively choose. But there are many good reasons to include some harder, faster sessions too. If steady running is the carbohydrate of running sessions, these faster sessions are the fats and proteins – essential, but needed in lesser amounts. Running at a greater intensity than you are accustomed to will raise your aerobic capacity, improve your technique, increase your leg turnover (the number of steps you take per minute), enhance your ability to tolerate and deal with lactic acid in your muscles, and increase muscle strength and power in your legs.

Threshold training also improves your running economy – the amount of energy needed to run at any given pace – and muscle fiber recruitment, so that you run more efficiently. One study found that adding threshold sessions into a distance running program for six weeks knocked two minutes off a 10K race time.

Try including one threshold run a week. Run at a pace at which you can't hold a full-scale conversation – just the odd curse or grunt – although it should be a pace you can initially sustain for perhaps 20–30 minutes. This is a great way of learning how to judge your pace and run at a constant speed. As you get fitter, you can increase the length of the threshold session, but don't increase it beyond about 35–45 minutes maximum. After that, work instead on increasing your speed.

While running harder takes you outside your comfort zone, it isn't as bad as it sounds, because you don't have to do it for prolonged periods. There are three main ways of increasing intensity: threshold training (running at a steady, fast pace for a given period), interval training (interspersing fast running with periods of jogging or rest), or running hills.

Threshold training

Steady, fast-paced running is known as threshold or tempo training. This is because it is done at a pace that has you teetering on the brink of what's called your lactate or anaerobic threshold (the point at which there isn't enough oxygen coming through to meet demand, causing a build-up of lactic acid in the muscle). Lactic acid and the acidic environment it creates play havoc with muscle contraction, which is why you sometimes get the feeling that your thighs have turned to jelly. However, the reward of working at this level is that it will gradually push your lactate threshold upward, so that you can run at a higher intensity without accumulating lactate in the muscles.

Interval and speed training

These sessions are about mixing bouts of speed with slower-paced running or even rest breaks. Interval training tends to mix fast bouts of running with jogging recovery, while traditional speed work usually allows complete rest between efforts.

The beauty this type of training is that it enables you to put in a lot of high-quality, fast-paced running without feeling either physically or mentally exhausted. This gets you used to working at a higher heart rate and effort level so that steady running feels easier. A study in *Sportscience* found that replacing some moderate-intensity endurance runs with interval training significantly boosted endurance. It'll also help you develop that all-important sprint finish!

CHANGING PACES

What do we mean when we say "comfortable" or "hard" pace? Well, because everyone is different, we can't say run at 150 bpm heart rate or run at 7 mph, as that may be nearly impossible for one runner and a piece of cake for another. There are a number of ways of monitoring your effort and pace.

A heart rate monitor allows you to keep track of your heart rate while you're running and allows you to set your own individual parameters of training based on your weight, gender, age and level of fitness. It's a great tool if you use it properly, although many runners just strap it on and then glance at it occasionally to see what their heart rate is, rather than using it actually to shape their session.

A simpler – and fairly effective – alternative is to use what's known as rate of perceived exertion (RPE). This simply means that you rate how hard you are working on a given scale. The beauty of this kind of self-rating is that it is truly individual, so you are working at your own level. Also, as you get fitter, your pace will quicken, so you'll be able to run a little faster – at, say, your level three. The original RPE scale, named after its inventor Borg, goes from 6 to 20 and can be a bit complicated. The scale below is a simpler alternative.

Level 1 – easy pace. Good for recovery runs and some of your slower long runs as well as during the "recovery" sections of hills, speed and fartlek runs. Equates to 60–65 percent of your maximum heart rate.

Level 2 – conversation pace. The one you want for your steady long runs. Equates to 65–75 percent of your maximum heart rate.

Level 3 – challenging pace. This is for threshold runs and hill work. Equates to 75–85 percent of your maximum heart rate.

Level 4 – tough pace. Use this pace on longer interval repetitions, such as 800 m to 1-mile repetitions. Equates to 85–90 percent maximum heart rate.

Level 5 – maximal pace. Use this pace on shorter interval reps and intervals only – with rests at least twice as long as the length of the effort. Equates to 90 percent or more of your maximum heart rate.

You can manipulate a speed session by varying the:

- intensity – the speed at which the effort is run
- length of the effort
- length of the recovery or rest interval
- volume – the number of efforts you put in

What you choose to do depends on your goals, your fitness level and experience. Some recent research by French sports scientists found that the ideal session for improving aerobic fitness is a ratio of three-minute work to two-minute recovery.

The obvious place to do speed work is an athletics track, but in fact, you can do it anywhere that is flat and free from traffic and obstacles, such as a park or soccer field. The treadmill is another option: It's easy to keep tabs on your speed and time, and there's no chance of slacking during the efforts, or you'll go flying off the back of the machine!

Fartlek

If you've never played around with varied-pace running, one of the easiest ways to start is to have a go at fartlek. Fartlek translates from Swedish as "speed play" and is a less formal way of incorporating faster bouts of running into your training. These bouts are traditionally determined by features of the landscape or street furniture, such as trees, benches or lampposts. For example, you might sprint between every second park bench, or you could start at a jog and accelerate a little more as you pass each tree until you are going flat out. Have a vague idea of how many efforts you are going to put in before you start so you don't risk the session being too easy or too hard.

Hitting the hills

Another way of upping the intensity of your runs is to hit the hills. The simple fact that you have to resist gravity to get up them means you are working harder. Uphill running uses 20 percent more muscle fibers than running on the flat, according to research from the University of Georgia, so it's fantastic for leg strength and power. If you are quite new to running and haven't experimented with any kind of speed training, it's best to kick off your higher-intensity work with hill training. In general, the idea is to run up the hill and then jog back down.

Alternatively, try a Kenyan hills session, in which you run continuously up and down the hill at a fast pace for a given period before resting and repeating. This combines hills with interval training and isn't for the faint-hearted, but it does get results. Focus on good technique – pumping your arms and taking slightly smaller, faster strides than you would on the flat. And make sure that you pick a hill that isn't so steep that it compromises your technique. The number of hill reps you do depends on the length and gradient of the hill and on your own fitness level and aims.

Pick 'n' mix

So those are the key running sessions that make up your training "menu." What you choose to do depends on what aspect of your performance you are focusing on. For example, if you're marathon training, you'll focus more on distance and less on speed. If you're trying to smash your 5K personal best, it'll be the other way around. But there should still always be more than one element in your training regimen.

The sum total of all your training sessions put together is known as your training volume. There is no magic number to tell you what an ideal training volume is: once again, it depends on your individual needs. However, there is some research to show that the benefits to be accrued beyond 50 miles of training a week tail off rapidly. In other words, there comes a point where more isn't necessarily better. But bear in mind that your volume of training needs to grow if you want to continue getting fitter as a runner (not necessarily by running more often or for longer, though – it could be a result of running harder). And also that the lower your volume, the longer it will take to make improvements. (That doesn't mean it's a bad thing, it's just that you need to be patient.) Also, remember that some people have a far higher threshold of training before getting fatigued or injured than others do.

Keep an open mind

Once you've formulated your running program, hopefully incorporating the principles outlined above, you have to be prepared to throw it all up in the air sometimes. You need to monitor your body's response to training and be ready to make changes where necessary. For example, if you have struggled with week three of a running program and are now meant to move on to week four – which is even harder – don't. Stick with week three, or even take a day out of the schedule to rest. It isn't a race. Being flexible about training isn't the same as being undisciplined. It's far more sensible to hold back from a punishing session if you don't feel ready for it than to grit your teeth and carry on. The important thing is to do what feels right for you. That's why you should never simply copy what someone else does. What works for them may be wholly inappropriate for you.

Final considerations

There are a few other factors to bear in mind when planning your training. Where are you running, in terms of what's underfoot? The variety principle comes into play again here – you don't want to do all your runs on the punishing surface of concrete. You can read more about surfaces on pages 51–53.

Also, what about the non-running activities you do? Remember when you are planning your running schedule to factor these in, otherwise you may unwittingly be following hard days with more hard days and failing to get sufficient rest and recovery. Read more about cross-training in chapter 8.

Finally, remember that what you are able to achieve from your running isn't just a matter of how much effort and time you are willing to put into training. It's also based on what your starting point is, in terms of your level of fitness, your age, gender and experience. They always say that athletes should choose their parents carefully, and it's certainly true that there is a strong genetic component to what can be achieved. But don't be disheartened. Most of us are a long way from our genetic ceiling and have many happy training hours ahead before we reach that lofty height. Just don't push yourself too hard to get there.

inner strength

a guide to core stability for runners

You've probably heard of core stability – it's a term that is frequently bandied about by runners – but what is it, and why is it relevant? And, more importantly, have you got any?

Put simply, the core comprises the "bits in the middle" of the body (the trunk and pelvic area) that are supported and stabilized by special muscles called "tonic" muscles, or "stabilizers." Their job is to maintain neutral posture and resist gravity, both at rest and during movement. The main core stabilizers are: the deep-set transversus abdominis (TA), a muscle that sits beneath your "six-pack" and wraps all around the midriff like a corset; the bottom or gluteal muscles (especially the gluteus medius); and the muscles of the lower back. Each has its own specific role, but collectively they act as a cylinder to stabilize the spine and pelvis.

At least, that's how they should act. But when these stabilizing muscles are weak or don't "switch on" when they need to, other muscles – known as phasic muscles – step in. Now, the usual job of these muscles is to facilitate movement, not stabilize, so this additional work can leave them short and tight, pulling the body out of alignment and leaving it more vulnerable to injury. Here's an example: If the gluteus medius isn't successfully stabilizing the hip, then the hamstrings – phasic muscles – step into the breach. Over time, this makes them shorter and tighter and more likely to tear, especially when you go for that sprint finish!

Although the main focus of stability exercise is the core, there are tonic muscles throughout the body. For example, a muscle in the thigh called the vastus medialis obliquus (VMO) keeps the kneecap in line, while the rotator cuff muscles stabilize the

shoulder blades. But let's focus for a moment on the stabilizers that keep the trunk and pelvis in correct alignment.

As you are reading this, sit up tall onto your "sit" bones, draw in your lower tummy and gently ease your shoulder blades back and down. Feel how much easier it is to take a deep breath? The core musculature is now working to support your posture, and the body is aligned as it should be. Now let yourself slump right down and let the tummy muscles go. If you take this poor posture into running (which many of us do, straight from work!), huge amounts of stress are put on the spine, both as a result of the motion itself and of the impact forces from landing. There is now clear evidence of a link between faulty movement patterns and muscle and joint pain, and core stability exercise is widely recognized as a vital step in preventing this kind of problem.

Assessing your core stability

How do you know if you have good core stability? Well, an absence of injury is one sign, if you've already been running some time. But the tests below will help you assess your core fitness.

1 Stand with your back against a wall, with feet approximately 7.5 cm away, hip-width apart. Try to lift one leg off the ground without tipping or sliding to one side, and without tensing up. The more stable and upright you remain, the better your core stabilizers are working.

2 Lie on your back, with knees bent and feet flat. Lift your pelvis off the floor, making sure the hipbones stay level with each other. Now, keeping everything still, straighten one leg without letting the bottom drop or the pelvis tilt to either side. You may find you can stabilize better on one side than the other.

Finding your level

However you fared in the tests, the good news is that you can improve your core stability. And in doing so, you will improve both your body awareness and your posture. So where do you start? There are two types or "levels" of core stability exercise: low load and high load. The goal of the low-load exercises is to improve posture and stability and to correct faulty muscular recruitment patterns so that you are putting minimal stress and strain on the body. These exercises teach the body to "switch on" the correct movement patterns and inhibit ("switch off") the overactive muscles that tend to step in as substitutes. They do this by establishing the correct neuromuscular pathways – the brain-to-muscle connections. As you might expect, the exercises are quite subtle.

High-load exercises, on the other hand, improve your ability to control the body in more demanding situations, such as when you are out running. Even if you are running well and injury-free, it's worth starting off with the low-load exercises if this type of work is new to you. The body has a great capacity for cheating and will try to use the phasic muscles instead of the stabilizers if the correct neural pathway hasn't been established. Even when you have progressed to the high-load routine, the low-level exercises can be done first as preparation.

The core basics workout

The following low-load sequence will activate your key core muscles. It is ideal to perform as a warm-up to switch on the muscles before your run, or you can do it first thing in the morning to set you up for the day. Because the "load" of these exercises is low, it is fine to do them every day.

1 Setting the core

Purpose: This is the most important of all the core exercises, as it builds the foundation for a strong core and teaches you how to "set" or "engage" the right muscles.

Starting position: Get down on hands and knees with hands below shoulders and knees below hips. Have your spine in a neutral position – neither arched nor rounded – and let the tummy relax and hang down.

Exercise: To engage the core, pull the pelvic floor muscles "up and in," and then draw up the lower part of the tummy, keeping everything else perfectly still. Hold for 10 seconds, breathing freely. Repeat 10 times.

Tip Contracting the pelvic floor should feel as though you are stopping yourself going to the toilet.

2 Bent-knee fallout

Purpose: This works on the hip stabilizers, aiding pelvic alignment in running.

Starting position: Lie on your back with knees bent and feet on the floor. Relax the ribs and engage the transversus abdominis (TA) by drawing in the lower tummy **(a)**.

Exercise: Let one knee fall slowly out to the side, while keeping the pelvis still and maintaining the TA contraction **(b)**. Don't allow the pelvis to rotate with the leg. Repeat 10 times and then swap legs.

Tip Place hands on the pelvic bones to detect any unwanted movement.

SARAH'S CASEBOOK

I ran a 10-mile race – it was the farthest I'd ever run at that pace. At 8 miles, my right leg was much more tired and achy than my left as a result of my core muscles being weaker on that side. If I were very brave, I'd include a picture here, showing how that side collapses, but it isn't a pretty sight! You'll have to take my word for it, and I'll be working on my core exercises . . .

a

b

3 Knee lift

Purpose: This works on stabilizing the pelvis while the legs move.

Starting position: Lie on your back with knees bent, feet flat on the floor and core engaged **(a)**.

Exercise: Pick one foot off the floor and lift the leg (keeping it bent). Stop lifting as soon as the pelvis starts to move or twist. Lower and repeat **(b)**. Repeat 10 times per leg.

Tip If it's hard to do this without the pelvis moving, start with both knees already lifted off the floor **(c)**. Then increase the lift on one leg until there is movement in the pelvis.

a

b

c

4 Clam

Purpose: To activate the gluteus medius, an important hip stabilizer, and "switch off" a hip muscle called the tensor fasciae latae (TFL), which can cause lots of problems when overactive.

Starting position: Lie on your side with your spine in a neutral position and the legs stacked **(a)**. Bend your knees to 90 degrees and your hips to 45 degrees.

Exercise: Keeping the feet together, lift the top knee approx 5 cm and hold for 10 seconds **(b)**. Repeat five times.

Tip Feel the muscle at the front of your hipbone, the TFL: try to keep this relaxed. If it starts to contract, lower the knee slightly.

a

b

The core challenge workout

If you perform the core basics routine before every run, you will be well on your way to greater core stability, better posture and a reduced risk of injury. But by building on this base of core strength, you can improve your running performance and reduce fatigue, too, by minimizing unnecessary movement, improving your running economy, enhancing stride length and improving neuromuscular efficiency.

The strength and stability you'll gain from the following high-load workout will help prevent the usual rocking and rolling of the spine and pelvis that occurs when fatigue sets in toward the end of a race or hard training session. (Who hasn't suffered in this way in the last quarter of a race?) Such unnecessary movement compromises form and pace.

This workout uses the same core stabilizing muscles as the core basics sequence, but this time the legs are working too, so the actions are more closely linked to running. You'll need a mat, a Swiss ball and a resistance band or tube. Aim to perform this workout three to four times per week.

1 Bridge
Purpose: An essential exercise for runners, this prevents "sitting" on the pelvis when running.

Starting position: Lie on your back with knees bent and arms resting on the mat, palms facing down.

Exercise: Slowly curl the spine up off the floor, starting at the tailbone, until the body forms a straight line from the shoulders to the knees **(a)**. Hold for 5 seconds, building up to 10 seconds. Repeat 10 times.

To progress: Perform the exercise as above, but once the pelvis is lifted, straighten each leg alternately, keeping the pelvis level **(b)**.

a

b

2 Plank

Purpose: To strengthen the deep abdominal muscles – along with many other muscle groups. This classic core exercise is done by all the elite training squads.

Starting position: Lie face-down on the floor, propped up on your elbows, with knees and feet together **(a)**.

Exercise: Engage the core and lift the hips and knees off the floor, taking the weight through your elbows and feet only, with the body in a straight line **(b)**. Hold for 10 seconds and repeat five times.

To progress: Perform the exercise as above, then from the extended position, lift one leg up, keeping the pelvis and back still and maintaining the straight line **(c)**.

a

b

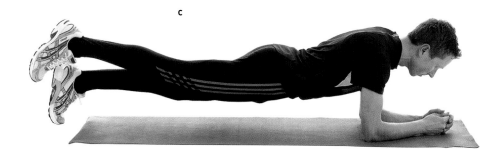

c

3 Kneeling hip extension

Purpose: This teaches controlled limb movement while maintaining a stable pelvis.

Starting position: Begin on hands and knees, with knees below hips and hands below shoulders, elbows straight. Keep your spine in neutral **(a)**.

Exercise: Extend one leg behind you and hold it out straight, keeping the back neutral and core engaged **(b)**. Hold for 10 seconds and repeat five times per leg.

To progress: When the leg is lifted, try to lift the opposite arm, keeping the body level **(c)**.

a

b

c

4 Ball squat

Purpose: This version of the squat maintains a stable core while working the quadriceps muscles at the front of the thigh.

Starting position: Stand with feet hip-distance apart, your back leaning on a Swiss ball against a wall **(a)**.

Exercise: Squat down by bending the knees, not allowing the back to arch or round **(b)**. Stop when the thighs are parallel with the floor and push back up. Repeat 20 times.

To progress: Perform the exercise as above, but with one leg lifted in front to add a balance challenge.

a

b

5 Crab walk

Purpose: To strengthen the glutes.

Starting position: Secure a resistance tube or band around your ankles so that there is some tension in the band when the feet are 20–25 cm apart. Bend your knees to about 30 degrees **(a)**.

Exercise: Take one leg out to the side, working against the resistance of the band, then join it with the other foot **(b)**. Take five steps one way and then go back in the opposite direction. Do five sets of 10 repetitions.

To progress: Perform the exercise with more resistance or increased speed.

a

b

6 Ball bridge

Purpose: To strengthen the deep abdominals.

Starting position: Sit on a Swiss ball and scoot back until you are lying on it, with feet flat on the floor.

Exercise: Walk the feet forward until the pelvis is not supported by the ball any longer, and hold this position for 10 seconds without letting the pelvis sag **(a)**. Repeat five times.

To progress: From the position above, lift one leg to as near the horizontal as possible, keeping the raised leg straight and the pelvis level **(b)**.

a

b

7 Leg lowering

Purpose: To strengthen the whole abdominal region.

Starting position: Start by lying on your back with the legs straight up in the air at 90 degrees. Keep the back flat on the ground to protect the spine **(a)**.

Exercise: Slowly lower the legs away from you until the back feels like it may start to lift, *but don't let it* **(b)**. As soon as you reach that point, bring the legs back up again. If this is too hard, try one leg at a time, keeping the other leg straight up.

To progress: Take the legs a little further.

a

b

Bear in mind that these workouts aren't a substitute for getting an individual screening to find your own weaknesses and be given a tailor-made prescription of exercises. However, they are a great starting point, and you'll see and feel the benefits quickly. Don't confuse or replace core training with traditional strength training, such as circuit training or weight lifting. This is a valuable and worthwhile addition to your training program – read more about it on page 86. Core workouts can, and should, be done at the same time to gain maximum benefit – and to ensure that your strength is more than skin deep.

cross purposes

making cross-training work for you

Many of us consider other activities as second-best alternatives to running. But incorporating other types of training into your program has much value – not only adding variety, but potentially enhancing performance, too.

The idea that something other than running can improve your running prowess shouldn't come as much of a surprise given how important core stability and stretching are, but, at the same time, the whole concept of cross-training flies in the face of specificity, one of those core principles of training. Surely to get better at something, the idea is to do lots of it? Well, yes, but there comes a point where upping your mileage may increase your risk of injury and muscle trauma more than it is worth, in terms of improved performance. But that doesn't stop you honing your aerobic performance, stamina and muscular endurance through other activities. A physical therapist or other sports medicine professional may have suggested that you intersperse running with other activities so that you reduce the overall amount of stress and impact on the joints. Cross-training enables you to work on different aspects of your fitness or performance without leaving you at risk of injury, burnout or overtraining.

Role play

Bearing that in mind, it's important to consider what role cross-training activities have in your running program, rather than just sticking them in for the sake of it. This ensures that you pick the right kind of activities, go about them the right way and work at an appropriate level of intensity. For example, a two-hour steady bike ride will help enhance your aerobic fitness and work on muscular endurance in the legs, rather like running, so this would count as a performance-enhancing cross-training session. By contrast, a gentle half-hour swim stretches out the muscles, takes the weight off the joints and doesn't raise heart rate into the training zone, so its role would be what we call "active recovery."

What's the alternative?

The purpose or role of the cross-training activity is what dictates the type of training that is most appropriate. As far as enhancing running performance is concerned, though, one activity appears to be particularly valuable: cycling.

Two wheels good . . .
The research on cycling as a cross-training activity for running is so impressive that the journal *Peak Performance* rates it the number-one alternative. In research conducted at the University of Toledo, Ohio, scientists asked 10 well-trained runners, who averaged 30–35 miles of weekly running, to add three cycle workouts per week to their existing schedules. After six weeks, perceived effort during strenuous running had fallen and their 5K times had improved by almost 30 seconds. Would adding three runs have created even better gains? The researchers put this to the test by getting a second group of 10 runners to add three additional runs to their 30–35 miles of weekly training. The fitness gains were the same. In other words, adding extra running training wasn't any better than adding cycling sessions in terms of producing faster running times. And the lack of impact meant that the cyclists were able to push up their training volume without increasing injury risk.

Work on your cardio

Other good alternative activities that place a similar demand on the cardiovascular system as running, without the musculoskeletal load, include the aptly named cross-trainer (elliptical trainer), which you'll find at most gyms. While various studies have found no significant difference in oxygen consumption, heart rate and calorie expenditure between treadmill runners and those using an elliptical trainer, research from Western Kentucky University found that, for the same output, rate of perceived exertion (RPE) was higher on the elliptical, because of the perceived higher intensity of effort from the leg muscles (in other words, you feel as if you are working harder, although you are not). As long as you don't mind that increased perception of effort, you can make equal gains in the same time period. Research from Dublin found similar fitness improvements after 12 weeks of training on a treadmill and an elliptical trainer. As far as impact is concerned, research from the University of Wisconsin found the elliptical trainer's impact rating is similar to that of walking, so a good deal less than running. To make your cross-trainer workout more running-specific, don't hold the handles – use your arms in a running action instead.

The stair-climber, another gym staple, can also be beneficial to running performance. One study found that runners who did only stair-climbing workouts for nine weeks were able to improve their running performance as much as subjects who continued to run. The real benefit here is the gain in quad strength, which will make tackling those hills easier. Step classes – and good old aerobics – also challenge your aerobic fitness and have the benefit of multi-directional movement: a nice change for your body from constant forward motion.

Be a sport

If you are more of a sports jock than a gym rat, ball and racket sports can have impressive crossover effects for running, and their stop–start nature makes them a good alternative to interval training. A soccer player typically covers around 10 kilometers during a 90-minute match, running at paces varying from a jog to a sprint and traveling in all directions. Games such as badminton and squash hone agility and speed. But bear in mind that you are still undergoing impact on the joints with running-based sports and that any contact sport leaves you vulnerable to injury risk (in other words, if you're in your final weeks of training for an important race, a serious soccer match isn't the best idea!).

Walk this way

What about walking? Well, it's less specific to running than you might think. Although you are putting one foot in front of the other, the cardiorespiratory load is lower, the impact less and the biomechanics slightly different. Walking works the "back" of the body more than running, using the calves and hamstrings to propel the body forward. Running uses much more of the front of the thighs, as the knee is bent more deeply when the foot is on the ground than in walking. Interestingly, there isn't a great deal of difference in

the calorie expenditure for walking or running a mile – a study in the journal *Medicine & Science in Sports & Exercise* found that the average energy expenditure for running one mile was 113 calories, while the average for walking it was 81 calories. But, of course, you cover the mile more quickly if you run.

Make it count

Make sure you factor your aerobic non-running activities into your program (by counting them as sessions), rather than simply adding them on to your existing running workload. Relating your cross-training to specific running sessions helps you plan your program, so you don't end up overdoing any one aspect of training. For example, in the University of Toledo study, the three cycle sessions that were added included two interval sessions and one 50-minute steady ride. It wasn't just three mindless bike rides! So think what kind of running session you are mimicking with each cross-training session you do.

This also ensures you aren't inadvertently increasing – or reducing – your training volume. If, for instance, you plan to replace a 45-minute moderate-paced run with a session on the cross-trainer or exercise bike, don't expect to get the same benefits from 20 minutes of coasting! Equally, if you play hockey on Saturday afternoons and always feel battered and exhausted the next day, don't plan to do your long runs on Sundays. It's a good idea to use heart-rate monitoring for cross-training sessions so that you can ensure the intensity matches up to your running efforts. Bear in mind that for non-weight-bearing activities, such as cycling and swimming, your calorie output will be lower than with running, as you are not carrying your own body weight. But also remember that just because you're an experienced runner, it doesn't make you automatically ready for the same volume of training in another sport, so approach new activities with caution and common sense.

Give me strength

It's not just cardiovascular activities that can enhance your performance in running. In fact, number two in the *Peak Performance* cross-training ratings – and an activity that is often neglected by runners – is strength training.

Far from making you bulkier and slower, increasing your strength is like adding another cylinder to your

car's engine. A study in the *Journal of Sports Medicine* showed an improvement of 8 percent in running economy following a period of strength training. Think what that could mean for your marathon time! American marathon runner Steve Spence allegedly increased his stride length from 70 to 73 in. (178 to 185.5 cm) after a year of heavy strength training. This saved him well over a kilometer of strides in his 2 hour 11 minute marathon. The improvements resulting from strength training are thought to be a result not just of physically stronger muscles, but also of more efficient neuromuscular pathways.

As far as injury prevention is concerned, strength training is immensely valuable because it makes not only the muscles, but also the tendons, ligaments and other connective tissues more robust. Strong muscles are better shock absorbers, so they can cope with the impacts of running better – especially downhill. In addition, strength work redresses the muscular imbalances caused by just running, such as an inequality between the strength of the quads and hamstrings.

No bones about it

There's the issue of bone health too. Research has shown that weight training can increase bone density, which is especially important for runners with a history of osteoporosis in the family, or for women who are approaching menopause (a time when levels of bone-friendly estrogen decline rapidly). Young female athletes who experience amenorrhea (loss of periods) are also at risk of poor bone mass due to low estrogen levels and should seriously consider strength training. Research in *Medicine & Science in Sports & Exercise* showed that strength training has a more all-around effect on bone density than normal weight-bearing activity, such as walking, which increases bone density only on the specific joints bearing weight.

Grow old gracefully

If improved performance and injury prevention aren't good enough reasons for you to get your hands on some weights, consider this: The average adult loses 5–10 percent of muscle mass between the ages of 20 and 50. The strength of the back, leg and arm muscles plummets by as much as 60 percent between the ages of 30 and 80; spinal extension range decreases rapidly; and ankle joints can lose half their range of motion between the ages of 55 and 85. Strength training can help halt the decline in muscle mass (which, sadly, running will not) and maintain mobility. And it's never too late to start – even people in their 80s and 90s have seen significant strength gains as a result of regular weight training. And the weaker you are, the easier it is to gain an improvement. Besides, if strength training is good enough for Paula Radcliffe, it's good enough for us!

Making strength training running-specific

● Since the goal is to improve fatigue resistance in the muscles and enable them to contract over and over again for extended periods, strength training for runners involves using a higher number of repetitions and lighter weights than if you were training for brute strength and muscle size.

● Don't focus just on the lower body. Running is a very repetitive sport and uses certain muscles constantly, others not at all. It is important to work the whole body and use the running muscles in different ways to create a more balanced regimen. Increased upper-body strength, for example, will help you get a greater contribution from your arm swing, which will aid your forward motion.

● Strength training can be done on your lighter running days or non-running days – but don't do it on consecutive days.

● Get an instructor or personal trainer to devise you a program, making sure that they know you are predominantly training to enhance your running. Or, once a week, try the circuit workout on the next page.

Runner's circuit

The following circuit consists of nine exercises. Do 20 repetitions of each one (10 on each side where applicable), and aim to complete three sets. If you want more of an aerobic challenge, pair up with someone and do step-ups while the other person completes the exercise before swapping.

Remember to warm up before you do the circuit (see pages 26–29).

SARAH'S CASEBOOK

When I trained seriously as a track athlete, a weekly circuit was an essential part of my training program. I used to go to the circuit session that Seb Coe attended when he was living in Sheffield in South Yorkshire. The legendary running coach, George Gandy, still runs a well-attended circuit session for athletes at Loughborough University in Leicestershire. Try to get your local running club to add a circuit night to training.

1 Lunge
Purpose: This is good for quad and glute strength.

Starting position: Stand with feet hip-width apart.

Exercise: Take one foot forward and bend the forward knee so the weight goes over the foot, allowing the back knee to travel toward the floor. Come back to standing and repeat on the other leg. Keep the pelvis in neutral.

2 Calf raise
Purpose: A great exercise for calf strength.

Starting position: Stand with the toes on a step and heels off the back edge (a).

Exercise: Slowly lower both heels so they are below the step, then rise up onto the toes (b).

a   b

3 Squat jump

Purpose: This is good for dynamic strength and muscular elasticity.

Starting position: Crouch down with the fingertips on the floor **(a)**.

Exercise: Jump up, stretching your arms above your head **(b)**, then crouch down again.

a

b

4 One-leg dip

Purpose: Improves stability and strength of the quads.

Starting position: Stand on one leg, with the other foot out in front.

Exercise: Bend the supporting knee to approximately 45 degrees, keeping the pelvis level. Do 10 on one leg, then swap to the other side.

5 Step-up

Purpose: This is good for lower-limb coordination and general lower-body strength.

Starting position: Stand in front of a bench, step or the bottom step of the stairs.

Exercise: Step up with one foot and follow with the other. Step down with the first leg and then the other. Do 10 leading with one leg, then swap to lead with the other.

6 Hamstring hack

Purpose: Builds strength in the oft-neglected hamstrings.

Starting position: Lie on your back on the floor with one leg resting on a step and the other leg in the air **(a)**.

Exercise: Keeping the pelvis level, push down on the supporting heel and lift the buttocks off the ground, then lower **(b)**.

a

b

7 Burpee

Purpose: Great for dynamic strength and muscular elasticity.

Starting position: Crouch down with your weight on both hands and feet **(a)**.

Exercise: Spring both legs backward until they are straight, keeping the weight on your hands **(b)**. Spring the legs back to the start position, then jump up into the air and return to the start position.

a

b

8 Squat

Purpose: This is a really good exercise for the glutes, hamstrings and quads.

Starting position: Stand with the legs shoulder-width apart, hands on hips.

Exercise: Slowly bend the knees, keeping the back straight and taking the bottom out behind. Bend to no more than 90 degrees, if comfortable.

Jump to it

Plyometrics is a specific form of strength training that has been shown to be particularly effective for runners. It makes use of something called the "stretch–shortening cycle" to train the muscles to fire more quickly and recruit more motor units so that they can respond more explosively and powerfully. In plyometric exercises, a concentric (shortening) contraction is immediately followed by a powerful eccentric (lengthening) one, such as a jump or hop. This coupling of contractions improves your ability to exert force at speed, making you a more powerful runner. One study, in the *Scandinavian Journal of Medicine and Science in Sports*, found that nine weeks of plyometric training improved a 5K time, even in well-trained distance runners. It's thought the improvements are a result of neuromuscular changes, allowing runners to run faster before hitting their anaerobic threshold (the point at which there is no longer enough oxygen coming through to meet demand). Other research from the University of Texas found that six weeks of plyometric training improved running economy.

Plyometrics isn't for the beginner, however – and you shouldn't attempt plyometric moves until you have already built a good base of strength. It's essential to maintain correct alignment and technique during plyometric exercises, to warm up thoroughly beforehand, and to start with just one simple session per week. Do not include it in your running program all the time; instead, introduce it once every 6 to 12 weeks.

9 Star jump

Purpose: A good exercise for working the muscles that facilitate lateral movement, which are often neglected.

Starting position: Standing with feet together and arms by your sides.

Exercise: Jump up, spreading the legs and arms apart and land with feet back together.

Plyometric workout

The following plyometric exercises should be performed in two sets of 10 repetitions, with complete recovery between sets. Don't increase repetitions as you improve – instead, increase the height, power or distance.

4 Jump off a step or bench with both feet **(a)**, and as you land go straight into a forward jump **(b)**.

a

1 Hop forward on one leg, aiming for height and distance. Swap sides.

b

2 Jump with two legs together, side to side, over a marker on the floor.

5 Do lunge jumps: start in a lunge position **(a)** and leap directly upward, switching legs in midair to land on the opposite side **(b)**. Continue to alternate from side to side for the set.

a

3 Jump with two legs together forward and back, over a marker on the floor.

b

Yoga and Pilates

Two other non-aerobic activities that have considerable benefits for runners are yoga and Pilates. Yoga used to be discouraged for runners, because it was believed it made them "too flexible," but now some yoga centers even offer specific classes for runners and the benefits are widely recognized. Such as? Well, increased flexibility is an obvious one, but yoga also enhances muscular endurance (from holding those postures), balance and coordination. It may even help your running physiology. A study published in the *Indian Journal of Medical Research* showed that athletes who practiced yogic breathing (*pranayama*) for a year were able to exercise at a higher work rate without increased energy demand or lactate production; while research in *Alternative Therapies in Health and Medicine* found that yogic breathing increased lung capacity and function. There's also the mental side of yoga, which can help hone mental focus and aid relaxation. A final benefit to consider is improved rate of recovery.

Pilates, developed in the early 1900s by Joseph Pilates, is a very precise, controlled series of exercises that focus on correct body alignment and usage, particularly on recruiting and working the deep abdominal muscles (the transversus abdominis and internal obliques), so it's great for the core.

SARAH'S CASEBOOK

I find that yoga works my body in ways and places that running doesn't target. It helped to strengthen my core and helped me discover areas where my range was limited and that I hadn't known were tight, especially rotational movements of the spine. Yoga practice also gives me quiet time, which allows me to relax and reenergize.

Some practitioners still follow Joseph Pilates' original method to the letter, while others have brought in more recent knowledge of the body and adapted the exercises accordingly. Many physical therapists are enthusiastic about Pilates, which suggests it has a potentially valuable role in injury prevention and rehabilitation, and indeed recent research from Queen's University in Ontario, Canada, shows that regular practice can reduce the incidence of lower back pain.

Pilates can be done in two ways. Studio classes utilize special machines (originally designed by Pilates himself), such as the "reformer" and "trapeze table," which are equipped with straps, springs and pulleys to facilitate muscle lengthening and strengthening. Or there are mat-work classes, which are predominantly equipment-free, perhaps using basic items such as blocks or pillows.

Cross-training for recovery

Cross-training isn't always about substituting alternative activities for running – it can be about aiding recovery from running. Research in the *International Journal of Sports Medicine* suggests that active recovery can aid lactate removal and improve subsequent performance better than completely passive recovery (like lying on the sofa), although it may be less beneficial as far as glycogen refueling is concerned. Just as you don't want to shirk those substitute cross-training sessions, you don't want to overdo your effort level in recovery cross-training. Working too hard when you are meant to be recovering is counterproductive.

Consider using low- or non-impact activities, such as swimming or cycling, to help your body recover and give it a break from the rigours of running.

Maintaining fitness during injury

Sometimes cross-training is simply a necessity. You're injured and you can't run, but you want to maintain your fitness as much as you can. One of the best activities for this is water running while wearing a flotation belt. It's not the most exciting activity in the world, but very valuable all the same. It closely resembles normal running and works the cardiovascular and musculoskeletal systems in a similar way. In fact, studies have shown that if water running is done correctly, aerobic fitness can be fully maintained. A study from the University of Toledo showed that trained runners who ran only in the pool five or six times per week over four weeks had no change in their 5K performance times. What's more, water running is compatible with most running injuries, because the water provides support. To get the technique right, try to stay upright, and drive with your arms and legs.

If you use heart rate as a gauge for training intensity, note that it will be 8–11 beats per minute slower in the pool than on land as a result of the temperature and pressure of the water on the body, which make the volume of blood pumped larger on each beat. The best way to train in the water is to mimic your normal training. Combine intervals, tempo training and steady running just as you would in a normal week, but concentrate on time rather than distance. Flotation vests are available from some sports shops and pools, but if you can't find one, ask your local physical therapist if you can borrow one.

Take a walk
Walking has less impact on the joints than running, and you may be able to walk without pain even when an injury has curtailed your running. A recent study reported that walking could prove useful in rehabilitation following a lower-body stress fracture, after an initial rest period of two weeks and a further two weeks of non-impact cross-training.

As far as other activities are concerned, the golden rule is to do whatever doesn't hurt, which will be dependent on the type and site of your injury problem. Cycling or the cross-trainer often work well for less serious injuries, as they challenge the musculoskeletal and cardiorespiratory systems without impact. If in doubt, always ask your physical therapist or doctor for advice.

chapter 9
food and drink
the role of good nutrition and hydration

What you eat and drink doesn't affect just your health and body weight – it also has a considerable influence on your performance as a runner and on your recovery. A healthy balanced diet, with sufficient calories and the right balance of carbohydrate, protein and fats is the bottom line, but the demands that running puts on the body mean there are some additional nutritional considerations.

So, that old chestnut, the healthy balanced diet: what exactly does it entail? And how do you know if you're getting one? The American College of Sports Medicine (ACSM) recently produced a paper on nutrition and athletic performance, drawing on the latest findings and beliefs. The recommendations are not exactly groundbreaking stuff – the key issues raised are sufficient energy and macronutrient intake (that's the big three: carbohydrate, protein and fat), sensible timing of meals and snacks to aid performance and recovery, and good hydration. Let's take a look at what all this means to you as a runner.

Energy intake

It's not possible to run on an empty tank. Even if you are trying to lose weight through running, you cannot simply deprive your body of the calories it needs. Insufficient energy intake (lower than energy output) results in fatigue, greater susceptibility to illness and injury and poor performance. It also has a detrimental effect on muscle mass and bone health.

People who are dieting, or who follow special diets or eliminate whole food groups, are at the greatest risk of nutrient deficiencies, according to the ACSM paper.

How, then, do you know that you are getting enough energy? Well, for moderately active adults aged 19–30, the US Institute of Medicine (IOM) suggests a daily intake of 2000–2200 calories for women and 2600–2800 calories for men. If you run regularly and consistently, it's likely that your individual requirements are higher than this, because you will be expending more through running.

A good way of gauging your running energy expenditure is to multiply your body weight by the distance run:

body weight (kg) x kilometers run (on a flat surface) = energy expended in calories

This calculation gives you a reasonable estimate, but it is not exact, and the figure will be higher if you run a lot of hills, as it relates only to flat surfaces. Also remember that you are an individual. Even if you and your partner or best friend do exactly the same training sessions, it doesn't follow that your energy or nutrient needs are the same.

SIGNS OF ENERGY UNDERCONSUMPTION

- Fatigue
- Weight loss
- Deteriorating performance
- Amenorrhea (ceasing of menstrual periods) in women
- Poor immunity (low resistance to illness and infections)
- Low bone density, if tested

The energy suppliers

Getting enough calories overall is paramount. But where should those calories come from? There are four different "suppliers": carbohydrate, fat, protein and alcohol (although alcohol isn't the best choice!). While all four can be used to produce energy, their energy potential varies.

Energy supplier	Energy per gram
Fat	9 kcal
Protein	4 kcal
Carbohydrate	4 kcal
Alcohol	7 kcal

Remember, however, that foods are not made up exclusively of one type of fuel but contain a mixture, say, of protein and fat, or carbohydrate and fat. The overall energy content (kcal value) of a food is the sum total of each component it contains.

Carbohydrate

We all know that carbs are the runner's five-star fuel, so hopefully your carbohydrate consumption falls at least within the IOM's recommended range of 45–65 percent of your total energy intake. A recent study of the dietary habits of elite Kenyan runners found that they consumed a staggering 76.5 percent of their calories in the form of carbohydrate!

But to know what percentage of each nutrient you are consuming means writing everything down, and then analyzing its content. Increasingly, experts believe it is more practical to determine nutrient requirements according to your body mass. The ACSM paper mentioned above recommends 6–10 g of carbohydrate per kilogram of body weight per day for regularly active people. So, for example, if you weigh 60 kg, you need between 360 g and 600 g daily. This is much easier to determine, as you can look at food labels.

THE FEMALE ATHLETE TRIAD SYNDROME

Some studies have shown an increased incidence of eating disorders in female athletes, often accompanied by poor body image, cessation of periods and bone loss: this is known as the female athlete triad. If there is insufficient calorie intake or excessive training, body fat drops below a certain level (which varies from person to person) and then menstrual irregularities develop, either irregular periods or amenorrhea (no periods at all). The problems associated with loss of periods are loss of bone density and the increased risk of stress fractures. There is also an elevated risk of osteoporosis developing in later life.

The American College of Sports Medicine recommends the following intervention within three months of amenorrhea starting:
● Reduce training intensity by 10–20 percent
● Gradually increase total energy intake
● Increase body weight by 2–3 percent
● Maintain daily calcium intake at 1500 mg.

Why is carbohydrate so good? Well, for starters, it's the only fuel that the brain can use. It also provides a readily available source for activity – stored in the muscles and liver in the form of glycogen. Carbs are also rich in B vitamins, iron, magnesium, chromium, fiber and phytochemicals (plant-derived nutrients) that can help prevent cancer and promote good health. For maximum benefit, however, you need to choose your carb sources carefully.

The glycemic index

Types of carbohydrate that release their energy slowly, such as brown rice, lentils and porridge oats, have what is known as a low glycemic index (GI), while highly refined starches, like white bread and rice, cause a sharp rise and subsequent fall in blood sugar and have a high GI. GI is a measurement of how fast and how high blood sugar rises after you eat enough of a food to provide 50 g of carbohydrate.

High GI foods can create energy peaks and troughs, causing you to snack unnecessarily or forgo runs because you feel tired, and too many of them increase the body's propensity to store fat instead of burn it. For these reasons, as well as the fact that, in general, low GI foods are healthier, try to make most of your carbs low GI.

Don't get too obsessed about it, though. Remember, a food's GI is based on eating enough of the food to get 50 g of carbohydrate, not 50 g of food.

Protein

Protein forms the fabric of our muscles, helps build and repair all the body's cells, regulates fluid balance and is a component of every oxygen-carrying red blood cell. Proteins are constructed from substances called amino acids, of which there are 20, all with distinctive functions within the body. Of these 20, eight are termed essential amino acids, because they must be supplied by the diet and cannot be made from other amino acids. If you are a vegetarian, you need to be sure that your protein sources provide you with all the essential amino acids by ensuring your diet is varied, including a range of dairy products, beans and legumes, soy, tofu, eggs and fish (if you eat it).

Do you need more protein if you're active? Experts used to believe not, but increasingly they recommend slightly more protein to very active people who have a higher lean body mass and undergo a greater amount of tissue damage, because protein is used in small amounts as a fuel during physical activity. While protein is not one of the body's major fuel suppliers – it prefers to use carbohydrate and fat – in some situations, such as when the muscle's carbohydrate stores have been used up, or when you aren't consuming enough carbs, protein can be broken down to produce energy.

Couch potatoes can get by on .8 g protein per kg of body weight daily, but the ACSM paper recommends 1.2 g to 1.4 g of protein per kg for men and women who do endurance training. However, before you go out to stock up on chicken breasts and eggs, bear in mind that most of us already consume more than enough protein.

Fat

Fat is significantly more fattening per gram than either carbohydrate or protein. It also requires little processing to be stored in the body, so there is a good chance that the fat you eat will end up in your fat cells, whereas 10–20 out of every 100 calories of carbohydrate and protein consumed are used for processing and metabolizing. That's not to say you should avoid fat, however. A fat intake equal to 20–25 percent of your overall energy intake is ideal – although a little lower than the IOM's recommendation of 20–35 percent. It's necessary to cut down your dietary fats if you want to shed body fat, but while all fats, from virgin olive oil to lard, contain the same calories gram for gram, they are not the same in terms of health.

Most of us get too much fat from unhealthy saturated and trans-fat sources (derived from meat and dairy products, pastry, fried food, cakes and biscuits) and not enough from healthier monounsaturated fat sources (such as olive oil) and omega-3 essential fatty acids.

The body is unable to manufacture the essential fatty acids omega-3 and omega-6, so we need to consume them regularly. With omega-6, we normally do – as it is derived from abundant seed oils, corn oil, nuts and seeds – but many of us skimp on omega-3, which is found in oily fish such as sardines, salmon, herring and mackerel. Consuming omega-3 fatty acids is thought to be protective against the thickening of artery walls, helping to make the blood less sticky and lowering blood pressure.

There are specific exercise-related benefits to be had from omega-3, too. Research has shown that it increases the delivery of oxygen to exercising muscles, optimizing your aerobic capacity, increasing your endurance and, ultimately, helping burn more body fat. There's also some evidence that it hastens recovery after hard training. If you aren't a fish eater, significant amounts of omega-3 can be obtained by eating certain nuts, including walnuts, linseed and its oils, and dark green leafy vegetables such as kale and spinach. Or you could consider taking a supplement.

Snacking and pre- and post-workout fueling

Healthy snacking is a great way of keeping energy levels constant and ensuring you don't fall short of your necessary calorie intake. That doesn't mean hitting the vending machine for a chocolate bar every afternoon, but opting for snacks that top up your nutrient levels, such as fruit and raw vegetables,

recovery. While some recent research has challenged the idea of a half-hour window of opportunity for replenishing glycogen stores, it is still important to get fluid and snacks on board as quickly as possible. The recommended content of your post-workout refueling snack is 1 g of carbohydrate per kilogram of body weight, but, in general, 50 g of carbohydrate is a good aim. Try a bagel with a little butter and honey.

Fluids

Every bit as important as what you eat is what, and how much, you drink. There's no doubt that being dehydrated is detrimental to performance – and, at extreme levels, to health – but some very recent research suggests that low levels of dehydration (less than a 2 percent loss of body weight, more correctly referred to as hypohydration) are not really a problem and won't necessarily affect performance.

nuts and seeds, smoothies and yogurt, and whole wheat bread or crackers with a protein topping, such as peanut butter or low-fat cheese.

Pre-run snacks

According to the American College of Sports Medicine, the ideal pre-run meal or snack should provide sufficient fluid to assist hydration, be low in fat and fiber, be high in carbohydrate and have moderate protein content. Given that, pre-run, you need energy quickly, it would seem sensible to make pre-workout snacks high GI, but the evidence on this is conflicting. While earlier studies favored high GI foods, researchers at Penn State University found greater benefit from a moderate-GI meal, compared to a high GI one, consumed 45 minutes before exercise. See what works best for you by experimenting with different pre-workout snacks.

Post-run snacks

Evidence suggests that your post-run refueling snack should combine protein and carbohydrate to enhance

While bodies such as the ACSM used to offer specific guidelines about how much to drink before, during and after a workout or run, their 2007 guidelines no longer do this, recognizing that the amount of fluid needed to stay adequately hydrated varies from person to person and from situation to situation, depending on the sweat rate of the individual, ambient temperature, intensity of exercise, clothing and humidity. Recent studies have shown that sweat rates can vary widely, ranging from .4 to 1.8 liters per hour during vigorous exercise.

What the ACSM does stress, however, is the importance of being adequately hydrated when starting your activity. "Prehydrating with beverages, in addition to normal meals and fluid intake, should be initiated when needed at least several hours before the activity to enable fluid absorption and allow urine output to return to normal levels," states the report. In other words, don't suddenly glug down a liter of water half an hour before your run!

You also need to maintain hydration when you are out on the run. But what should you drink? Experts recommend that for longer sessions (45 minutes or more) you opt for an isotonic sports drink, containing 6–8 percent carbohydrate per 100 mL along with electrolytes (sodium and potassium salts lost through sweat). Studies are fairly conclusive on the benefits of sports drinks over water during endurance exercise, but water alone will help you stay hydrated and is better than nothing at all.

How do you know how much fluid you need?
Weigh yourself before and then after (naked and toweled down) a timed run during which you take no fluids. An hour or half hour is easiest to calculate from. See what the difference in your weight is before and after. You can assume that this is all fluid loss, with 1 g of body weight equating to 1 mL of fluid. For example, you may find that you have lost 1.5 kg of body weight during an hour-long run. This would equate to 1500 mL of fluid. On future runs, you should aim to drink at least 80 percent of the amount of fluid your body has lost.

Rehydrating
Once your run is over, don't forget to rehydrate. You will recover much more quickly if you make fluids part of your recovery strategy. Keep drinking, little and often, until your urine is the color of pale straw. Is water adequate? If you are eating a carbohydrate-based snack, yes. But if not, then a sports drink, with carbohydrate and electrolytes, is preferable. A study from the Chinese University of Hong Kong compared performance in a run to exhaustion following a 90-minute run and a 4-hour recovery period, in one instance with full hydration with a sweetened placebo and in the other with an isotonic carbohydrate-electrolyte drink. In the second run, run time was, on average, 24.3 minutes longer after the carbohydrate drink, even though rehydration was achieved in both trials. The trial was double blinded too, so subjects

didn't know what they'd drunk. It's fairly compelling evidence for the benefits of sports drinks on recovery – but such recovery is probably not necessary after a half-hour jog around the block. Proprietary sports recovery drinks normally contain a little protein alongside the carbs and electrolytes.

Supplements and ergogenic aids

There's still a lot of debate over whether active people need to supplement their diet with extra vitamins, minerals or other supplements – and, indeed, whether doing so will enhance performance, aid muscle gain or weight loss, or hasten recovery. The issue of ergogenic aids (performance-enhancing substances) is still one where rumor and anecdote are far more common than solid scientific evidence. A report by the University of Washington concluded that, for endurance runners, the only true (and legal) nutritional ergogenic aids were water, carbohydrate and caffeine – all available in your local grocery store!

The caffeine fix
We've already looked at the benefits of carbohydrate, but what about caffeine? Tests at the Australian Institute of Sport in Canberra found that athletes who took a small quantity of caffeine could exercise up to 30 percent longer than those who took a placebo.

More specifically, caffeine improves performance and endurance during prolonged, exhaustive exercise. One study showed that it was able to delay fatigue in a treadmill run to exhaustion, while other research has found that it can improve endurance performance by 10–15 percent. How? Most probably by lowering your perception of effort so you don't feel you are working as hard. Other theories include the idea that caffeine enhances your neuromuscular pathways, so muscles fire more efficiently. It also improves concentration, reduces fatigue and increases alertness. According to a study in *Current Sports Medicine Report*, caffeine is relatively safe and has no known negative performance effects, nor does it cause significant dehydration or electrolyte imbalance during exercise.

So how much caffeine do you need? A report in the journal *Sports Medicine* states that doses of 6 mg per kilogram body weight are ergogenic, and you don't have to down gallons of coffee to benefit: for a 70 kg person, just three cups a day will do the trick. However, there is some research to suggest that caffeine taken in tablet form is absorbed more quickly.

Running-related supplements

Conjugated linoleic acid

There has been some recent interest in conjugated linoleic acid (CLA) as an ergogenic aid for endurance athletes. This is an omega-6 fatty acid, and research suggests it may be able to increase the rate at which we burn fat, increase muscle mass and inhibit fat storage. Sounds like magic, eh? But the findings are equivocal. One research project showed that 1.8 g per day, combined with 90 minutes of exercise three days a week for 12 weeks, resulted in an average 20 percent decrease in the percentage of body fat. Other research, from Kyoto University, concluded that CLA ingestion increased endurance exercise capacity by promoting fat oxidation during exercise – but, unfortunately, this study was on mice. A spate of more recent human studies have failed to demonstrate significant benefits, and a review in the journal *Nutrition* concluded that the effects of conjugated linoleic acid on body weight loss in humans were far less clear than those observed in animal studies. This is one you need to make up your own mind on.

Creatine

While there is evidence to support the use of creatine in repetitive sprint sports and strength training, there isn't much to support its use in prolonged aerobic activity. A study in *Medicine & Science in Sports & Exercise* found that supplementation had no effect on endurance running performance, though it did improve lower-body maximal strength, and performance in maximal repetitive upper- and lower-body high-power exercise bouts in repeated sprint performance.

Another study in the *Journal of Strength and Conditioning Research* showed that supplementation did not improve performance or rate of perceived exertion in interval running on a treadmill, compared to a placebo.

One way creatine might be useful, however, is in recovery. In a study in which runners who took part in a 30K race received 20 g of creatine or a placebo a day for five days prior to the race, the creatine reduced cell damage and inflammation after the race. It's worth bearing in mind that creatine use is often associated with increased body mass (not great for distance runners), cramping, water retention and diarrhea.

Glucosamine sulphate

This is a popular supplement among active people as well as those with joint pain not related to exercise, such as sufferers from osteoarthritis, and the research on it is fairly promising. Glucosamine is a protein-based compound that occurs naturally in the body. For best results, it is taken in conjunction with chondroitin (which also occurs naturally, in and around the cartilage cells). The combination of these two compounds appears to be able to improve mobility and reduce pain, mainly in the knees and hips. In one study, from the University of Western Australia, athletes experiencing regular, chronic knee pain took glucosamine supplementation or a placebo for 12 weeks (2000 mg per day). Eighty-eight percent of glucosamine takers reported some degree of pain relief, improved mobility and improvements in their pain levels after 12 weeks, compared to 17 percent who unknowingly took the placebo. A review of 15 other studies also concluded that treatment with either glucosamine or glucosamine plus chondroitin was effective in easing osteoarthritis of the knee. Studies suggest you need daily doses of at least 1000 mg of glucosamine and 800 mg of chondroitin and that you need to take them for several weeks before you notice the effects. There is no evidence to suggest that long-term use reduces effectiveness, and many athletes choose to take them preventatively, rather than as a treatment.

SARAH'S CASEBOOK

One of the sprinters I look after says he always knows when he's forgotten to take his glucosamine, as his knees start to ache!

Vitamin and mineral concerns

As far as vitamins and minerals are concerned, if you have a balanced diet with lots of variety you should get all you need and supplementation should not be necessary. That said, there's no harm in taking a good quality multivitamin and mineral supplement as backup, and it's definitely recommended if your diet leaves a lot to be desired. Tut tut!

Do runners and other highly active people need more of specific vitamins and minerals? Probably – but their increased calorie intake should cover this requirement. Here's the latest thinking on what you might need more of . . .

Antioxidants

Antioxidants are compounds that prevent, or attenuate, the process of oxidation in the body (this is the same process that turns an apple brown when it is exposed to the air). There is much evidence that strenuous exercise increases levels of oxidation in the body, leading some nutritionists to recommend that highly active people get more in their diet. Luckily, this isn't too difficult, as most fruits and vegetables are packed with antioxidants. Which ones? Those that are rich in vitamins A, C and E, along with the mineral selenium – so think carrots, red peppers, strawberries, oranges, avocados, blueberries and pomegranates. Make an effort to get your antioxidants from dietary sources – but consider supplementing, too.

Also, don't worry that you are doing yourself "damage" by running. Running might increase your body's production of "free radicals" (substances resulting from oxidation), but it also enhances your body's ability to soak them up and its ability to cope with these potentially harmful chemicals, says the American College of Sports Medicine.

Calcium

Calcium has many uses in the body, including an important role in facilitating muscular contraction, but the main concern as far as dietary deficiency is concerned is a detrimental effect on bone health. Calcium is one of the major building blocks for bone, and insufficient intake can lead to insufficient bone being laid down and an increased rate of bone loss.

Dairy foods are by far the most abundant source of calcium in the Western diet, but for those who do not eat dairy foods there are other good sources – including tofu and other soy products, and tinned fish (such as sardines or salmon). A recent year-long study found that increasing calcium intake through diet, rather than supplementation, protected bone density in women taking oral contraceptives. The Institute of Medicine's recommended daily intake of calcium for women aged 19–50 is 1000 mg. For women aged 51–70, this increases to 1200 mg per day. Women who are pregnant, breast-feeding or amenorrheic (whose periods have stopped) may also need higher-than-average intakes, and calcium supplementation is recommended for people recovering from stress fractures or fractures.

Iron

Iron deficiency is quite common among active people as a result of increased sweating, increased hemolysis (disintegration of red blood cells as a result of stress on capillaries) and, sometimes, insufficient dietary intake due to special diets. In a study of dietary intake of elite female athletes in Greece, micronutrient intakes were all found above the recommended values with the exception of iron. Red blood cell turnover is significantly higher in runners, compared to sedentary people, leading to an increased likelihood of iron deficiency. There is also a type of hemolysis specific to runners, known as foot-strike hemolysis, in which the red blood cells break down as a result of the "mechanical trauma" of foot strike. One study, in the *Journal of Applied Physiology*, found that overall hemolysis was four times as great after an hour of running compared to an hour of cycling, and the researchers speculate that this occurs because of the repeated foot strike on the ground in running.

You don't have to be anemic to be suffering from iron deficiency. According to research in the *Current Sports Medicine Report* in 2005, iron deficiency can present a whole range of symptoms from severe fatigue to adverse effects on performance. Iron is particularly important to women, because of the amount that is lost during menstruation. A study from Cornell University found that women who were iron-deficient, but not anemic, adapted less successfully to aerobic training than women who were given iron supplementation during the training period.

If possible, up your iron intake through diet rather than supplementation. The best sources (most easily absorbed by the body) are hem iron sources, which are meat and meat products and some seafood (oysters are one of the best sources). Non-hem sources are eggs, milk, vegetables, grains, legumes, seeds and other plant foods. Also look for iron-fortified foods, such as breakfast cereals and juices. Avoid drinking tea when you consume iron, as it hampers absorption, and include a source of vitamin C with non-hem iron sources in your diet to maximize absorption.

If you feel you may be at risk of iron deficiency, ask your doctor for a blood test to assess both ferritin and hemoglobin levels or take an iron supplement for a short while to see if it makes you feel any better.

chapter 10

injury time

what to do when you get hurt

Most of this book is about preventing injury – but what if you are unlucky enough to get hurt? How do you know what's wrong, what you should do to limit the damage, and if, or when, to see an expert? You'll find the answers to these questions here, along with specific information and advice on each area of the body and the injuries most commonly affecting it. But to aid your understanding of what to do and why, it's useful to know a little about the "running body."

What gets injured?

It really is true that your knee bone's connected to your thighbone, as the old song goes! It's known as the "kinetic chain." This means that each part of the body, from head to toe, is part of the same chain and that a problem in one area can be caused by – or cause – problems in another. To stay injury-free, the whole kinetic chain needs to be functioning properly. The body is linked not just by bones but by different types of connective tissue, including skin and muscle, as well as the circulatory and nervous systems. Let's take a closer look at the most important structures and at the kind of injuries they might sustain.

Bones are the body's structural support, withstanding all the impact and forces that we undergo. As far as injuries are concerned, bones can be broken (fractured) by falling or impact, or can sustain "stress fractures,"

which are micro fractures resulting from repetitive physical loading – either by impact forces being absorbed at one specific point or from the repetitive pull of a muscle. Stress fractures are most common in female athletes who have become amenorrheic (lost their periods), as the accompanying loss of estrogen makes bones more fragile. A stress fracture should be taken seriously, as it can develop into a complete fracture if not addressed.

Joints are the body's crossroads, connecting one bone to another, via **ligaments**. The ends of the bones are covered with articular cartilage to provide cushioning. It is this type of cartilage that is worn away in osteoarthritis. The joint is sealed with a capsule and lubricated by sticky stuff called synovial fluid, which also provides nutrition to the joint. Movement squeezes synovial fluid into the articular cartilage, which is why it's important to take joints through their full range of motion. If, for example, you never take the knee into full flexion, the parts of the surface that don't come into contact can degenerate more quickly.

The most common joint injury is a sprain, such as a twisted ankle or knee ligament. A sprain is classified into one of three grades:
Grade 1: A minor sprain that can be resolved in a couple of days.
Grade 2: A lot more pain and swelling and more fibers disrupted – taking longer to heal.
Grade 3: Complete rupture – normally requiring surgery.

RESTORING STRENGTH

Once a joint has been damaged, it is important to work on restoring strength in the surrounding muscles afterward. It takes only 5 mL (a teaspoon) of fluid caused by swelling to switch off the muscles that give the joint its protection.

Muscles are the workhorses of the body. They receive information from the brain, which tells them to contract, and, by pulling on the bones, muscles facilitate movement. Injuries to muscles are usually strains or pulls and, again, can range from a minor strain to a complete tear of tissue.

Acute tears occur as a result of sudden or explosive activity, while chronic muscle tears are generally a result of overuse and are among the most common injuries seen in distance runners. Picture the muscle fibers as fraying rope, which bleeds a little, then heals as scar tissue. As the scar tissue is tighter, it can then retear, becoming inflamed and developing a knot in the muscle.

While ligaments connect bone to bone and provide stability to a joint, **tendons** connect muscle to bone – such as the patella tendon, which attaches the quadriceps to the tibia via the kneecap, or the Achilles tendon, which attaches the calf muscles to the heel bone. Tendons consist of tight parallel bundles of collagen fibers that are built to transmit a lot of forces. Most ligament injuries are acute, while tendon injuries are more commonly caused by overuse or misuse. Tendonitis refers to inflammation of a tendon; tendonosis entails degeneration of the tendon.

The **nervous system** is the internal communication system of the body, running from the brain all the way to the toes. The nerves are encased in a sheath, called the dura, which protects them. The nerves run around joints and through various muscle interfaces and can be affected by injuries to other parts of the body. For example, if there is bleeding in one of the hamstrings, the sciatic nerve (which runs alongside) can also become stuck and tethered to the surrounding tissue. Nerves can also cause pain in a different place from where the actual problem is, which is a phenomenon called "referred pain." Referred pain usually originates from the spine.

Nerve symptoms include pain and pins and needles or numbness, and sometimes muscle weakness. Nerve pain should always be investigated by your doctor, and not ignored.

How injuries happen

Now that we know what can be damaged, let's examine how. Injuries tend to fall into two categories. Acute injuries are the ones that happen quite suddenly, and which you are immediately aware of, such as spraining your ankle or tearing a hamstring muscle. Chronic injuries, on the other hand, creep up on you gradually, so it's difficult sometimes to pinpoint exactly when or how they started. Because of its repetitive nature and the fact that it continually stresses specific areas of the body, running is more commonly associated with chronic injuries than with acute ones. Problems like tendonitis and iliotibial band syndrome fit into this category.

Chronic injuries

Chronic injuries are the bane of many a runner's life. They creep up on you without you really noticing, put a stop to your training and generally take much longer to settle than they did to arrive – or, at least, it seems that way. But the truth is, we are continually stressing certain areas of the body through running, and every runner's body has its own threshold point beyond which one or more structures or systems may break down. Unfortunately, there's no way of knowing what your individual threshold point is, so a problem can develop seemingly out of the blue when, in fact, it has been building up over a period of time. While an increase in speed or distance is often what pushes someone over the threshold, it can also simply be a result of the gradual accumulation of the same forces applied on the same areas of the body, time after time (that's why we keep telling you to add variety to your running surfaces and training sessions!).

Keeping a training diary is invaluable in helping you try to identify what went wrong and why, so it's worth routinely recording how you feel during and after your runs, noting any glitches, particular fatigue or tightness. But once you've got a chronic injury, what can you do to make it better?

Taking action – chronic injuries

It is very important to treat a chronic injury seriously: don't simply try to run through it or ignore it. While it may only just have started to cause you problems, it has probably been building up over a period of time and needs some recovery assistance. Follow the advice below to help reduce inflammation and pain.

Once you've done that, the next step is to identify the likely cause of the problem and rectify it, which the pages in this section will help you do.

● **Rest** The first action to take is to do nothing! In other words, rest the sore area for a couple of days.

● **Ice** can help reduce blood flow to the injured part and ease inflammation. Use for eight minutes at a time, twice daily. Ice any sore areas after training, too. See box opposite for how to ice an injury.

● **Anti-inflammatories** can help to settle down, in cases of chronic injury, the reaction in the area and allow the body to heal. Ibuprofen is effective, or you can get stronger drugs prescribed by your doctor.

● **Mobilize** the area to prevent it seizing up. If it is a muscle, try gently stretching it and the surrounding muscles to release some of the tension held there. If it is a joint, gently take it through its full range of motion.

● **Massage or self-massage** is worthwhile, especially if you can feel a thickened area in the tissue.

● **Arnica** is a homeopathic remedy believed to help with inflammation. Many physical therapists use an arnica-based massage cream. You can also take it orally, available from drugstores and health food shops.

● **Review your recent training** Have you increased your training volume suddenly? When were you first aware of the injury as even the faintest nuisance? Should you have rested after a hard race instead of pushing on with training? Look for any possible causes.

● **Look at your running shoes** The wrong shoes, or worn-out shoes, can contribute to injury problems. See chapter 4 for more information.

Getting help
If none of the above helps and the injury has persisted for more than two weeks or compromised your

training, seek help. If you try to train through pain, other areas will compensate and cause further problems. It's much easier to resolve an injury caught early than one that has been ignored until the body loudly protests. See "Who does what?" (page 114) to decide what type of expert help you need.

Acute injuries

You don't have to slip on a banana peel to sustain an acute injury. A sudden burst of speed can provide enough force to tear a hamstring; an uneven surface can cause a sprained ankle . . . Whatever the culprit, an acute injury occurs when the force put through a structure (a bone, ligament, muscle or tendon) is too great, causing it to give way, tear or rupture.

Taking action – acute injuries

The first 48 hours

What you do in the first 48 hours is vitally important, as acute injuries tend to respond best to early treatment and can develop into ongoing, chronic problems if left untreated. Put the RICE protocol into action as soon as possible, particularly in the case of a tear (see "How to RICE an injury," right).

During the first 48 hours is when the body's "inflammatory response" occurs – a defensive mechanism causing swelling, pain and heat to protect the injured area. Recent research from South Africa shows that for successful healing and a lower risk of re-damage, it is best to allow this response to happen naturally and not prevent it by taking anti-inflammatories too soon. Take non-anti-inflammatory painkillers (such as Tylenol) during this time, if necessary, and avoid any deep massage over the injured area.

After 48 hours

Once the crucial first 48 hours are over, start stressing the injured area through movement and stretching. This tells the newly generated cells where to go and what "shape" to take. If you keep the area

HOW TO RICE AN INJURY

REST: Immobilize and take weight and pressure off the injured area as soon as possible.

ICE: Apply ice – or even cold water – as quickly as possible to decrease the temperature of the area and limit further bleeding. Keep a disposable instant ice pack in your training bag. Otherwise, use crushed ice or a bag of frozen peas wrapped in a dish towel (don't put ice directly onto the skin). Ice for eight minutes every three hours, or thereabouts – more frequently than you would for a chronic injury (see opposite). Even though you might feel tempted to comfort yourself with a hot-water bottle, never apply heat to an acute injury: this will actually increase blood flow to the area.

COMPRESSION: Strap the area to compress it, prevent further damage and limit the amount of bleeding. It is worth keeping a gauze bandage in your equipment bag to strap an injury immediately.

ELEVATION: Elevate the area, if possible, so that blood flows away from the injury. For example, raise your leg above hip height.

Continue with your RICE measures for 48 hours to help form a stable wound. The quicker all of this is put into practice, the better the healing. Incidentally, it is rest and ice that are really crucial. There is limited evidence that compression and elevation help, but they still tend to be seen as good practice, as they help rest the injured area and take the pressure off it.

immobilized, the new tissue will form knots instead of smoothly aligned fibers, which can cause problems later on. Movement doesn't mean making the area hurt – all actions should be gentle and pain-free, and if necessary you can now take anti-inflammatories for five to seven days.

Get it moving

If you have a joint injury, start by taking it through its full range of motion. For example, with an ankle this would entail forward, backward and side-to-side movements and rotations.

If you have a muscle injury, your first priority is some gentle stretching – scar tissue is very inelastic, so it's essential to regain, and then maintain, mobility. Initially stretch only up to the point of pain, and then gradually creep further into the muscle's range of movement to stretch the scar tissue gently. You can also strengthen the muscle, at first just by using the weight of the limb – for instance by sitting down and straightening the leg out in front, or standing up and extending the leg out behind you. Gradually progress to weight-bearing exercises, particularly those that mimic real-life actions like running: these are more functional for rehabilitation than exercises that isolate a specific muscle.

Resume activity when it doesn't cause you any pain – but be aware than any post-exercise pain is a sign that you've overdone it, so you need to ease off a bit. It is important to have a structured rehabilitation program, rather than just randomly trying things: your recovery will be quicker if you work consistently on rehab exercises and keep tabs on your progress. Once you are ready to run again, see chapter 11 for advice on getting back on track successfully.

Getting help
If an acute injury is not easing after 48–72 hours, see a sports-medicine professional to ensure things are progressing as they should be and that something more serious hasn't been missed.

Who does what? Sports-injury experts explained

Emergency room
Go to the hospital only if you suspect a broken bone or an unstable (collapsing) joint and need an immediate x-ray or immobilization. If a joint is badly damaged, a referral to an orthopaedic surgeon will normally be made in the fracture clinic.

Primary care physician
Your doctor can give you advice on what is injured and should be able to suggest the next appropriate step. He or she may prescribe anti-inflammatories, should they be appropriate, and can refer you for further investigation, if required. Depending on your medical insurance, you may need a referral if you want physical therapy or to see a consultant.

Sports medicine specialist
Sports medicine specialists work privately and are usually linked to clinics and private hospitals. They specialize in diagnosing sports injuries and often have access to a diagnostic ultrasound machine so they can look at the soft tissues involved. They can also offer non-invasive therapy, such as the following:
● Anti-inflammatory injections using cortisone
● Homeopathic anti-inflammatory injections
● Injections of hyaluronic acid, which replaces the fluid within a joint. This is good for joints that have some wear and tear in the articular cartilage (the lining of the bone).

Physical therapists
Physical therapists are trained to diagnose and treat injuries and prescribe a rehabilitation program. They treat the body as a whole, working at the cause of an injury and looking from the spine and nervous system to the area involved. They may use a combination of manual therapy, electrotherapy – such as ultrasound or interferential – and exercise therapy.

Podiatrist
A podiatrist is a foot doctor – but that doesn't mean they can deal only with black toenails and heel pain. They also look at the effect foot strike has on the body's mechanics and are a good point of contact for gait-related problems. This is also who you need to see if you're advised to have orthotics made.

Chiropractor

Chiropractors are concerned with the alignment of bones and the effect it has on the spine, the nervous system and the joints. They use high-speed "adjustments" to restore function and movement to a problem area.

Osteopath

In osteopathy in the UK, trained osteopaths work with their hands using a wide variety of treatment techniques to deal with bone and joint problems (especially back pain). These may include soft-tissue techniques, rhythmic passive joint mobilization or the short, sharp "thrust" techniques designed to improve mobility and range of movement of a joint, similar to those of a chiropractor. (Note: In the US, the field of osteopathic medicine is very different – US osteopathic physicians are licensed medical doctors and surgeons who are qualified to practice the full range of medicine.)

Sports massage therapist

A sports massage therapist is best for general tightness, aches and pains rather than injuries per se, but is also useful as a preventative measure and to aid recovery. Sports masseurs are not qualified to diagnose injuries, but they are able to spot and iron out areas that feel very tight or knotted, which can be injuries waiting to happen.

Whoever you see, ask about their credentials, and ensure they are registered with the relevant governing body or organization.

Getting the most from your sports-injury expert

● Take your training diary with you to help you explain more precisely what led up to the injury.
● Make notes during the consultation – you may not remember that it was your piriformis in spasm, or a weak multifidus at the root of your problem, once you've left the clinic.
● If you are given exercises to do, make sure you

know exactly how to do them. Ask the doctor or physical therapist to write down how many and how often and, ideally, to draw stick figures showing how to do the exercise.
● If possible, find a specialist who is either a runner or who treats runners. They are likely to keep abreast of the very latest techniques and research in their favored area. Ideally, see someone recommended by another runner.
● Make sure you get to the root of the problem. Of course, your main priority is healing the injury, but making sure it doesn't happen again is equally important and is dependent on the specialist determining what caused it in the first place.
● Do what you're told! There is no sense in paying good money for expert advice if you don't heed it.

A note on the symptoms maps

The rest of this chapter is divided into six sections, each dealing with a different part of the body. The "symptom map" at the start of each section is an at-a-glance guide to the likely causes and "quick fix" treatment of common running problems. Follow the arrows to find the most likely diagnosis of your symptoms and turn to that heading for more details.

The back

Eighty percent of the population will suffer from back pain at some point in their lives, and sadly runners are no exception. Your spine is the very foundation of your running body. If its position is incorrect, forces are not distributed evenly along its length, creating tension and stress on the spinal structures, affecting all the muscles and joints of the pelvis and legs, and altering your biomechanics.

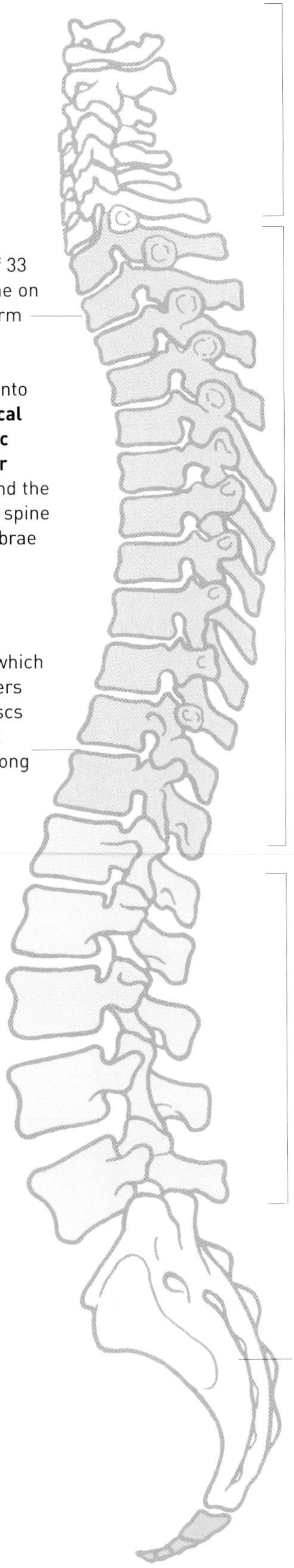

The spine consists of 33 **vertebrae** aligned one on top of the other to form a loose S-shape.

The spine is divided into four areas: the **cervical spine** (neck), **thoracic spine** (trunk), **lumbar spine** (lower back) and the **sacrum**. The lumbar spine consists of five vertebrae known as L1–L5.

The vertebrae are separated by **discs**, which act as shock absorbers for the spine. The discs consist of 80 percent water and have a strong fibrous outer layer.

cervical vertebrae

thoracic vertebrae

lumbar vertebrae

sacrum

The vertebrae are connected on each side by a **facet joint** that prevents excessive rotation and extension. However, if the facet joints are stiff, then extension (arching backward) will be limited – this is very common in runners.

The spine is supported by long and short **ligaments** at the front and back of each vertebral body.

The **spinal column** protects the **spinal cord**, from which all the body's nerves emerge.

Each nerve supplies the muscle control, sensation and pain of each body part: for example, the **sciatic nerve**, the largest in the body, supplies the back of the leg and is the one most commonly damaged in runners.

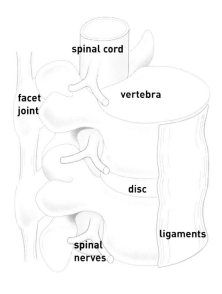

The spine is supported by small stabilizing muscles called **multifidus** and large phasic (moving) muscles called **erector spinae**.

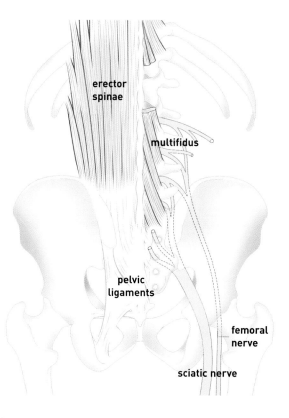

back pain symptoms map

(see note on page 115)

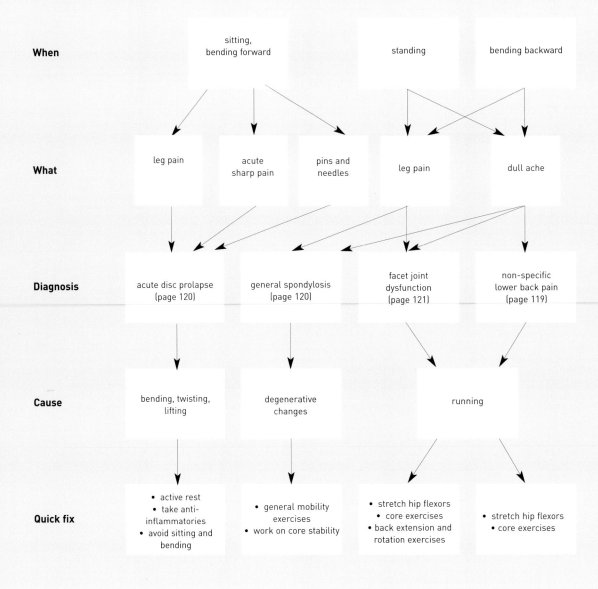

When

sitting, bending forward

standing

bending backward

What

leg pain

acute sharp pain

pins and needles

leg pain

dull ache

Diagnosis

acute disc prolapse (page 120)

general spondylosis (page 120)

facet joint dysfunction (page 121)

non-specific lower back pain (page 119)

Cause

bending, twisting, lifting

degenerative changes

running

Quick fix

- active rest
- take anti-inflammatories
- avoid sitting and bending

- general mobility exercises
- work on core stability

- stretch hip flexors
- core exercises
- back extension and rotation exercises

- stretch hip flexors
- core exercises

Non-specific lower back pain

The most common runner's back problem is non-specific lower back pain. This normally presents itself as a non-acute pain – aching on one side, both sides or centrally. The back often feels tight, and certain movements are painful, depending on the structure or structures affected. Movement is usually restricted at the end of the range, and there may or may not be associated hamstring and gluteal pain.

As its name suggests, it can be very difficult to pinpoint the exact cause of non-specific lower back pain. It is often a combination of problems, rather than just one – such as an inflamed disc, tight facet joints and tight muscles – which combine to restrict function and alter biomechanics.

So what are the most common causes of non-specific back pain in runners? Principally, muscle tightness or imbalance and incorrect running technique. Tight hamstrings, for example, pull the pelvis out of line and load the spine incorrectly, while overpronation increases pelvic rotation and tilt. Poor running posture – either "sitting in the bucket" or having an over-tilted pelvis and excessively curved lower back – can contribute to back pain. This can result from poor technique or fatigue. Weak abdominals and gluteals are another common factor, because they cause the hip flexors to tighten up. These, in turn, pull on the upper lumbar facet joints, causing them to stiffen and become inflamed. This then overloads the lower lumbar joints, creating irritation on the sciatic nerve that can make your hamstrings and calves take on a tightness that doesn't go away with stretching.

What to do
It is difficult to get an exact diagnosis for chronic lower back pain, but addressing tightness and weakness of muscles in the surrounding area will often resolve the problem. And, encouragingly, most spinal pain resolves spontaneously within three months.

SARAH'S CASEBOOK

The biggest predictor of back pain is having had previous back pain – in other words, your spine is weakened. That's why it's so important to strengthen the spine, following an injury or an episode of back pain, with core exercises and back mobilizations.

To tackle the symptoms, use a heat pack to relax some of the tight muscles (but note that these are not the cause of the pain). Don't have a hot bath, though, as the position you lie in when in the bath loads the spinal ligaments and makes them stretch further. Try a warm shower instead.

Anti-inflammatories will help settle the inflammation, while mobilization of the sciatic and femoral nerves (see pages 40–41) will prevent any adhesions forming as a result of the inflammation.

As soon as you are able, start the gentle back mobilization exercises on pages 122–123 and the core program on pages 74–81. Stretch the hip flexors, hamstrings and quads (see pages 37–38). Finally, reassess your running style, training volume and footwear.

If none of the above tips helps, seek advice, as you may need some assistance in realigning the spine and mobilizing the joints.

WARNING!

If you experience back pain with bladder or bowel weakness, muscle weakness, numbness in the legs or sudden unexplained weight loss you should seek medical advice.

Slipped disc (acute disc prolapse)

Non-specific lower back pain may be the most common back problem, but the most talked-about one is surely the slipped disc. A disc "slips" either when the spine has been under prolonged postural strain, such as from incorrect sitting, or following a sudden movement, like bending or twisting. The pulpy, soft middle part of one of the intervertebral discs bulges out and presses on the nerve, causing referred pain anywhere from the thigh to the foot. You'll know if you've slipped a disc, because you won't be able to move, and you'll have acute leg pain, sometimes accompanied by nerve symptoms, such as pins and needles and numbness. Any weakness in the leg, such as being unable to lift the ball of the foot off the ground, means the nerve is severely compromised, and you should seek medical advice.

What to do
See your doctor as soon as possible, who will probably prescribe painkillers and anti-inflammatories. Don't even *think* about running! But also avoid bed rest or staying in one position for too long. Try easy walking if pain allows and avoid flexion-based postures, such as sitting or driving, which will further load the disc.

Reclining in a hot bath will further stress the disc and ligaments, so a shower is a better idea. There is normally associated muscle spasm and neural (nerve) irritation with lower back pain, which can be eased with a hot pack (muscle spasms are normally a secondary sign of lower back pain, however, and not

SARAH'S CASEBOOK

A friend was getting a numb foot every time she ran. Pressing on her lower back was tender, although she was getting no pain in her back. I showed her some basic nerve mobilizations and quickly mobilized her spine, and she stopped getting a numb foot immediately. All this was done on a school bench!

the primary cause of pain). A cold pack can help to settle any inflammation around the disc: try both and see which you get most relief from.

Once you are taking steps to relieve pressure on the disc and decrease inflammation, address the strength of the muscles supporting the spine. Start the basic core program on pages 74–75 once any acute pain has settled. You can even do the first exercise from the core basics workout while pain is still acute.

Have a thorough assessment from a sports medicine professional, who will combine manual therapy with a suitable exercise program to aid rehabilitation.

Spondylosis

Spondylosis is a classic example of how one problem leads to another. The process starts when, as a result of wear and tear on the spine, the discs lose some of their fluid and compress, overloading the facet joints and causing them to stiffen up. This increases the wear on the discs. The body compensates by growing new bone cells on the edges of the vertebral bodies, called osteophytes, which stiffen the spine still further. Eventually, the space that the spinal cord and nerves occupy can become smaller, putting pressure on them and causing leg pain when you run and walk.

The symptoms of spondylosis are similar to those of non-specific back pain, but the condition is quite prevalent among older runners, so if you are past the first flush of youth and you are getting pain in one or both legs while running, see your doctor for an x-ray.

What to do
Take anti-inflammatories if necessary, and try to keep the spine and the muscles surrounding it as mobile as possible – see the back mobilization exercises on pages 122–123 and the basic core program on pages 74–75. You can run with spondylosis, but you would be wise to do low-impact cross-training on days when your back is very stiff.

Facet joint dysfunction

Facet joint dysfunction is one of the most common problems among runners – and even more prevalent in runners who cycle as well, because both activities load the facet joints. The problem stems from tight hip flexors, since these muscles attach to the upper lumbar facets (L1, L2 and L3): when they are short and tight, they pull the joints tight, too. Stiff facet joints mean limited extension, which compromises running technique and gluteal activation.

Facet-joint dysfunction tends to manifest itself as pain during or after running, tightness in the front of the hips (with poor hip extension) and pain in the lower back, normally on one side of the spine.

What to do
A good physical therapist will be able to mobilize the facet joints, easing a lot of the stiffness and reducing pain. But to prevent the joints stiffening up again, you need to work on spinal mobility – particularly extension and rotation (see the exercises on page 122).

The other crucial thing is to stretch those hip flexors. See the Thomas stretch on page 39 and practice it two to four times per day. It's also worth starting the core program (pages 74–81) to strengthen the abdominals and take excess stress off the spine.

Stress fractures

Stress fractures are most commonly seen in young runners (especially those who overtrain) and amenorrheic women, but this doesn't rule out the general runner completely. Spinal stress fractures can result from too much mileage, or a sudden increase in mileage. Pain is usually felt around the site of the fracture, or sometimes manifests itself as repeated hamstring strains, because the hamstrings are trying to protect the weakened spine.

The area that most frequently becomes stressed is the pars interarticularis. This is a small part of the

vertebral bone that links the facet joints to the vertebral body. If left untreated, it can fracture completely on one or both sides of the spine, leading to instability of the vertebral column and a "forward slip," known as spondylolythesis.

What to do
If you suspect a possible stress fracture, try this test: stand on one leg and lean backward – pain on one side may indicate a stress fracture. You should get an accurate diagnosis via a bone scan, which will tell you what stage the stress fracture is at and give you a better guide of how long to rest. During this period of rest, maintain as much spinal mobility as possible by doing the exercises on pages 122–123. Focus more on regaining flexion than extension initially. (If a spondylolythesis is diagnosed, extension exercises should be avoided: concentrate on flexion-based moves, such as hugging the knees to the chest.)

Start the basic core program (pages 74–75), and, once you can do it comfortably, try the more advanced exercises (pages 76–81). The glute ones in particular are essential. Strengthening the core helps to prevent any further movement and shear (twisting) forces on the disc, which can cause associated disc pain.

Stretch all the structures around the spine, especially the hamstrings and hip flexors.

There will be no running until the bone has healed, so get into a good routine of cross-training, ensuring there is no impact.

SARAH'S CASEBOOK

I treated an elite athlete who had spondylolythesis and who has continued to compete at the highest level. She has been extremely diligent with her core work and kept her hip flexors free, stabilizing the condition.

Back mobilization program

These basic spinal mobility exercises will help relieve any stiffness, maintain good range of motion and preserve healthy joints. If you have any back problems, doing the exercises as part of your warm-up allows as good an alignment as possible prior to running. Do each one five times.

Warning
These should not be done if you have acute lower back pain, any numbness or pins and needles or acute sciatic pain referred down the leg. Seek advice if you have any of these symptoms.

1 Lumbar rotation
Starting position: Lie on the floor on your back.

Exercise: Pick up one knee and take it across the body to the floor **(a)**, keeping the opposite shoulder on the floor.

To progress: If this is comfortable, straighten the leg and turn the head toward the opposite arm **(b)**. Repeat on the other side.

2 Back extension
Starting position: Lie face-down on the floor.

Exercise: Push up onto your forearms or straight arms (depending on how flexible your spine is – it doesn't matter if you can't straighten your arms, as long as you keep your pelvis on the floor). Hold for five seconds and slowly lower.

3 Curl
Lying on your back, hug both knees into your chest. Hold for 5 seconds and release.

a

b

4 Cat stretch

Starting position: Start on all fours on the floor, taking the weight through the hands and the knees.

Exercise: Arch the back, lifting the head and sticking the bottom out **(a)**. Think about lengthening rather than compressing the vertebrae. Then do the opposite movement by rounding the back as much as possible, tucking the bottom under **(b)**. Repeat five times.

a

b

Five ways to avoid running-related back pain

1 One of the biggest causes of lower back pain in runners is tightness of the psoas muscle (the major hip flexor). This muscle is repeatedly shortened during running. It originates from the top of the lumbar spine L1–L3, and when tight, it pulls on these joints, stiffening them up and overloading the bottom lumbar joints L4 and L5. Practice the Thomas stretch on page 39. Religiously!

2 If you have been sitting down all day, allow a transition period before running. Sitting loads the joints and discs of the back, which makes them less efficient at absorbing the impact of running. If you can, spend a few moments lying on the floor on your back with knees bent.

3 Ensure you have good posture when sitting to minimize stress on the spine. Sit up tall on your "sit" bones, draw in the lower tummy and draw your shoulder blades back slightly. Maintain a nice S-shape curve with your spine. If you are prone to disc irritation, it may be worth using a lumbar roll when sitting to prevent slouching.

4 Avoid any heavy lifting immediately after a run. This is because the discs have considerably less fluid in them post-run and are more vulnerable to injury.

5 Maintain your core strength. Performing some core exercises prior to running helps switch on the core muscles, which helps to maintain correct spinal alignment when you are running.

The hip and pelvis

The pelvis is an integral part of the kinetic chain for runners, as it transmits all the forces from the feet and legs to the spine. If the pelvis, and its associated musculature, are not correctly aligned, problems can occur up and down the body.

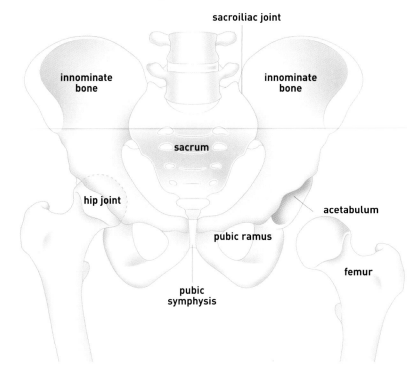

The pelvis is a bony ring protecting all the lower internal organs and providing structural stability via strong ligaments and sturdy joints. It consists of the **sacrum** and two **innominate** (unnamed) **bones**.

The bones are joined at the front by the **pubic symphysis** and at the back by the two **sacroiliac joints**.

The pelvis is joined on each side to the leg by the **hip joint**, an articulation of the head of the **femur** (thigh bone) to the **acetabulum**, a socket in the lower part of the innominate bone.

The **pubic ramus** is an area that may suffer a stress fracture.

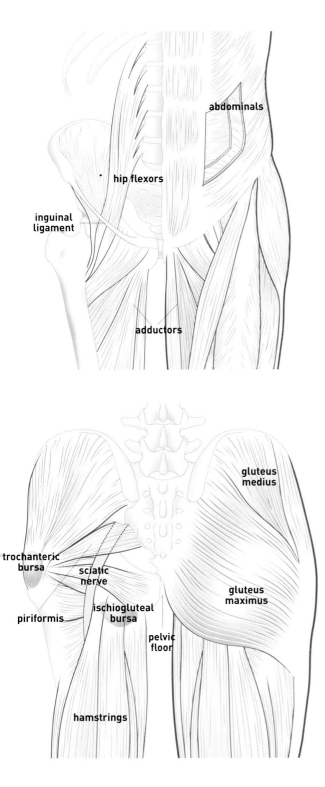

The pelvis is supported by a complex system of muscles and fascia (strong connective tissue, which connects one area to the next) – tightness in any of these structures can cause stress or misalignment.

The muscles directly overlying the pelvis are the **abdominals**, **hip flexors**, **gluteals**, **hamstrings** and **adductors**.

The hip flexors are one of the key areas for runners, frequently becoming very tight as a result of repeated contraction of the muscle, causing decreased stride length and tightness or impingement over the front of the hip.

The abdominals are connected via the **inguinal ligament**. In men this has a small hole through which the spermatic cord runs, making them more vulnerable to hernias.

The **gluteus maximus** is the largest muscle in the body and should be the runner's workhorse.

There are several bursae around the pelvis. These are small fluid-filled sacs that reduce friction as muscles move against the bones, and they can become inflamed. The **trochanteric bursa** sits underneath the **gluteus medius**, while the **ischiogluteal bursa** sits under the hamstring origin.

A small muscle called the **piriformis** sits underneath the gluteals and controls rotation of the hip joint. This can become inflamed and put pressure on the sciatic nerve that runs directly below it.

The groin is the area around the front of the hip.

The **pelvic floor** muscles form a sling at the bottom of the pelvis and co-contract with the deep abdominal muscles.

hip and pelvis pain symptoms map (see note on page 115)

Where	buttock	back of thigh	central anterior pelvis	front of the hip	groin/inside thigh
When	running	sitting	standing on one leg	mornings after running	squeezing knees together
What	local or referred pain	local tenderness	ache	non-specific pain	sharp pain
Diagnosis	sacroiliac joint dysfunction (page 127)	piriformis syndrome (page 127)	hamstring tendinopothy (page 133)	oseitis pubis (page 128)	hip joint (page 128)
Cause	• sudden jar (e.g., off curb) • overstriding downhill •repeated stress	• overuse • poor biomechanics • tight abductors • fast downhill	• speed work • short, weak hams • poor glutes	stiffness of the pelvis	• overweight • tight hip flexors and spine
Quick fix	stretch & strengthen hip flexors, glutes & hams	• ice • massage • avoid downhill • stretch glutes	• ice/anti-inflammatories • stretch & strengthen hams & glutes	• rest • stretch abductors •abdominal exercises	• stretch hip flexors • anti-inflammatories

The last column (adductor tendinopathy):

Diagnosis	adductor tendinopathy (page 135)
Cause	• tightness of adductors • uneven slippery ground
Quick fix	• stretch abductors • core • mobilize lower back

Sacroiliac dysfunction

The sacroiliac (SI) joint, at the back of the pelvis, is prone to injury as a result of the forces that it has to absorb and transfer during running. It can be directly damaged by a fall or sudden step off a curb, but more commonly problems are caused by repeated stresses pulling it slightly out of line, such as overpronation, weak hip stabilizers or poor spinal mobility. The pain is felt on and around the joint itself, or can be referred to the buttock and back of the thigh area or sometimes the groin region.

Once the joint is misaligned, the wrong muscles are recruited during running, compromising technique and causing misalignment and imbalances elsewhere in the body. A misaligned SI joint can also cause a functional leg-length difference (in other words, an apparent, rather than a genuine, difference in length), which obviously affects the gait cycle. Overstriding and running downhill can both place excessive strain on the joint.

To check whether your SI joint is out of alignment, place your hands over the two bony prominences at the base of the spine: they should feel level and even. Now lift each leg in turn, bringing the knee up in front. The movement under your thumbs should feel equal on each side as the leg is lifted. If one side fails to move, or moves a lot more than the other, there is likely to be a rotation on one side.

What to do
The principle line of treatment for SI-joint dysfunction is to stretch and strengthen the muscles around the pelvis, particularly the hip flexors, gluteals and hamstrings. To make it running-specific, your exercises should include some balance work on each leg, keeping the pelvis level. The core program on pages 74–75 is a good place to start.

If running is painful, avoid it – running with the pelvis out of line could cause other problems. At the very least, modify your training and use ice and anti-inflammatories to help settle down the inflammation locally. If the pain is acute, a sacroiliac belt may help to support the joint. Ask your physical therapist about getting one. When you are pain-free, return to running cautiously (see chapter 11 for more advice).

Piriformis syndrome

The piriformis is a small muscle in each buttock that externally rotates the hip. Piriformis syndrome occurs when this muscle becomes tight and inflamed. This can put pressure on the sciatic nerve that runs directly under the piriformis (or, in some people, through it), so you feel deep buttock pain or referred pain in the back of the leg, occasionally including pins and needles or numbness. You'll probably have pain not just when running but also when sitting, climbing stairs and squatting. The classic pain hotspot is the area of the buttock where the top of your jeans pocket would be. You may also have trouble internally rotating the hip.

Tight adductors and weak abductors are a common cause of piriformis syndrome, as this combination of tightness and weakness causes the hips to rotate, overloading the muscle. Poor biomechanics that internally rotate the hip, such as overpronation, can also be to blame, as can tight hip flexors. Running causes include too much running on a slanted surface and excessive downhill running.

What to do
Ice the area, and massage it using a golf ball. The easiest way to do this is to sit on the ball and roll around until you find the painful spot. This is a form of "trigger point" release massage. Modify your training to avoid downhill running, and be careful not to overstride. Stretch the piriformis using the gluteal stretch on page 36 – but modify it by drawing the knee of the stretching leg across the body. Also stretch the adductors and hip flexors (pages 36–37).

Osteitis pubis

The pubic symphysis is a joint at the front of the pelvis. It is a very stiff structure, joining the two bones by a fibrocartilaginous disc. Osteitis pubis is inflammation of this area, including bony edema (swelling). It starts as a vague groin pain, which makes it easily confused with other groin injuries, but it is normally painful directly over the pubic bone when the knees are squeezed together and when taking the body weight on one leg (as in running).

So what causes it? It can be a result of stiffness of the pelvic structure and spine, or weakness in the adductors and abdominals.

What to do
Initially, modify training so that there is no pain. This may mean complete rest, cross-training or reduced running, depending on the severity of the pain.

Stretch the adductors to remove any tension, along with the hamstrings and hip flexors, and start an abdominal-strengthening program. Try the core workout, but also include classic abdominal exercises, like crunches and sit-ups (curling the upper body off the floor from a lying position with knees bent and feet flat on the floor) to strengthen the rectus abdominis (the six-pack muscle).

Stress fractures

A stress fracture in the pelvic area is not a common injury, but any pain around the pelvis that isn't easing, and that gets worse with running, needs to be checked out, so seek advice. The most likely sites of damage are the pubic rami and the neck of the femur.

What to do
The most important step is to see a professional, because stress fractures in this area are tricky to diagnose. Rest is paramount, and you should do only impact-free cross-training. As a guide, recovery normally takes six weeks.

Hip pain

Runners can suffer from general wear and tear in the hip joint, particularly if there has been a previous injury to the area or if there is an external risk factor, such as being overweight. This usually presents as a stiffening of the joint, particularly in the morning.

The major hip flexor, the iliopsoas, is often over-worked by the repetitive nature of running. It can become short and tight, causing anterior hip impingement (inflammation of the joint capsule and surrounding structures). There can be inflammation of the bursa underneath the psoas muscle, causing a deep-seated pain in the hip, or associated lower back tightness and stiffness of the upper lumbar facet joints, from which the iliopsoas originates.

Pain that radiates from the front to the side of the hip, or "catches" as the leg is pulled toward the chest or the hip rotated, needs further investigation. Recent studies have shown that a lot of persistent hip and groin pain comes from within the joint. It could be a labral tear (that is, of the cartilage that deepens and stabilizes the socket of the joint), the joint capsule may be inflamed, or there may be an impingement of the hip joint (when the bone is pulled too far into the socket by tight muscles or connective tissue).

What to do
If you have a non-specific pain at the front of the hip area, stretching out the hip flexors and lower back are the first steps to take. Stretch the hip flexor in the Thomas position (see page 39) and mobilize the femoral nerve as shown on page 41. To maintain or redress the balance of the pelvic muscles, practice the clam (see page 75) and bridge (see page 76) exercises.

A nagging stiffness can be addressed with anti-inflammatories as well as stretching the hip flexors and mobilizing the lower back before and after running. Also ensure that you regularly take the hip through its full range of movement to feed the articular cartilage and prevent further wear. Remember, the hip goes forward and backward and rotates in its socket. Consider cross-training to avoid too much impact on the hip joint. Supplements of glucosamine with chondroitin (see page 104) have shown promising results in alleviating joint pain. If you suspect a more specific problem, avoid any flexion-based exercises that load the front of the hip joint (such as squats or rowing) and seek advice. Surgeons are now able to do arthroscopies of the hip to look inside and see what is causing the pain.

Lateral hip pain

The abductors are the muscles that take the leg out to the side and work hard in running to keep the pelvis stable. The main abductor is the tensor fasciae lata (TFL), which sits on the outside of the thigh at the top. This muscle is very prone to overwork if the gluteus medius isn't working properly. The TFL and gluteus medius can also become inflamed from overuse, causing local pain on the outside of the hip. Biomechanical problems, such as overpronation, can be to blame, as they create an imbalance between the two muscles, causing the TFL to work overtime and the gluteus medius to switch off. If the TFL is tight, it also pulls the iliotibial band (ITB) tight, which can lead to pain at the front of the knee.

SARAH'S CASEBOOK

A runner had vague pain in the gluteus medius region after a 10-mile road race and was unable to train. As it had not settled after a couple of weeks of cross-training, ice and anti-inflammatories, we looked at her gait and found a distinct lack of hip extension. Following a regimen of hip flexor stretches and lower back mobilizations, she was able to run pain-free again.

What to do
For local pain on the outside of the hip, use ice and anti-inflammatories and massage the area with an arnica-based cream. Then assess your core strength, and begin the core program on page 74. The clam exercise in particular is good for teaching your body to recruit the gluteus medius instead of the TFL. If the TFL is tight, use the Thomas stretch, then try to stretch further by taking the knee in toward the other leg. You'll probably need some help to do this!

Hernias

There are two forms of hernia, and you should see your doctor for an accurate diagnosis. A normal hernia is where a lump is felt in the groin region after heavy lifting, and which needs a surgical repair.

A sportsman's hernia is a weakness of the abdominal wall caused by overload. There may be an underlying weakness in the abdominal musculature, or the area can be overloaded as a result of tight structures, such as the adductors, putting extra stress on the region. There may be some pain on running, but the pain is more commonly felt afterward, and when coughing and sneezing. A sportsman's hernia is more common in men, as the spermatic cord passes through the inguinal ligament, causing a weak spot. If the abdominal wall is disrupted, it can pull on and inflame the ilioinguinal nerve and cause pain around the lower abdomen and groin and into the testes.

What to do
Stretching the hip flexors and mobilizing the nerve in the adapted Thomas position (see page 41) can help ease the symptoms. The core musculature needs to be as stable as possible to prevent further strain on the area. Follow the program on pages 74–81.

If the pain settles and isn't affecting your running and daily activities, carry on. However, if it's getting worse or not settling, surgical repair may be an option. See your doctor or a sports-medicine professional for advice.

The upper leg

The upper leg is dominated by two big muscle groups, the quadriceps and hamstrings, which respectively cover the front and back of the thigh. The adductors run along the inside of the thigh.

Back of leg

The **femur** is the long bone in the thigh.

The main muscles over the thigh are the **hamstrings**, **quadriceps** and **adductors**.

The hamstring group consists of three muscles: the **semitendinosus**, the **semimembranosus** and the **biceps femoris**. The hamstrings cross two joints – the hip and knee – and are involved in both hip extension and knee flexion, sometimes both at once. This means they are quite prone to breakdown, either because of an acute tear or chronic overload.

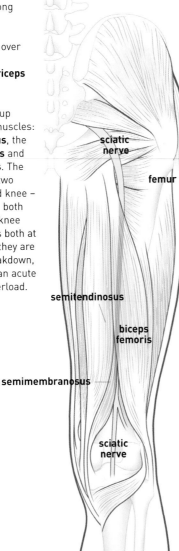

Front of leg

The **quadriceps** is the muscle group on the front of the thigh and, as its name suggests, comprises four muscles: the vastus group (**vastus medialis**, **vastus intermedius** and **vastus lateralis**) and the **rectus femoris**. The rectus femoris originates from the pelvis, while the vastus group originates from the top of the thigh. The main role of the quads is to extend (straighten) the knee, which is why they contain the **patella** (kneecap).

Pain originating from the spine is often referred to the upper leg, as the large **sciatic** and **femoral nerves** run down the back and front of the thigh, respectively.

The strength ratio of the quads to the hamstrings should be at least 80 percent, the quads being the stronger. The ideal ratio is 1:1, but most runners have weaker hamstrings because of the dominance of the quads in running.

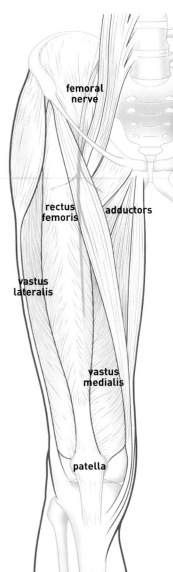

upper leg pain symptoms map (see note on page 115)

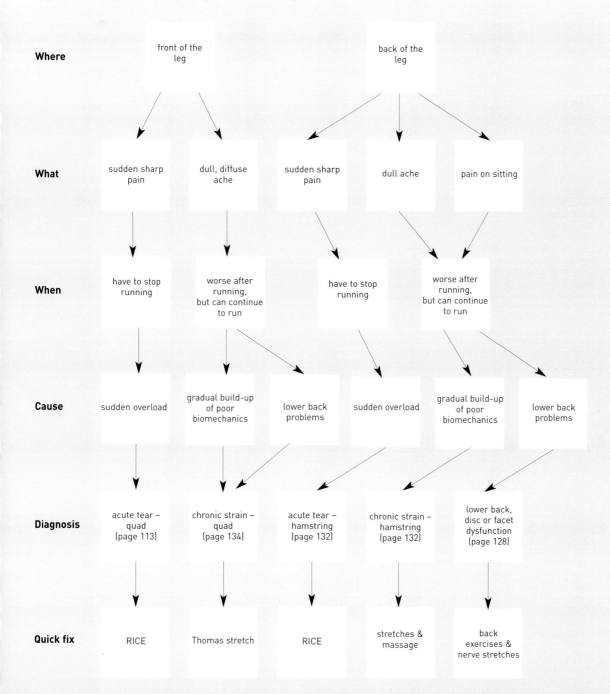

Where

front of the
leg

back of the
leg

What

sudden sharp
pain

dull, diffuse
ache

sudden sharp
pain

dull ache

pain on sitting

When

have to stop
running

worse after
running,
but can continue
to run

have to stop
running

worse after
running,
but can continue
to run

Cause

sudden overload

gradual build-up
of poor
biomechanics

lower back
problems

sudden overload

gradual build-up
of poor
biomechanics

lower back
problems

Diagnosis

acute tear –
quad
(page 113)

chronic strain –
quad
(page 134)

acute tear –
hamstring
(page 132)

chronic strain –
hamstring
(page 132)

lower back,
disc or facet
dysfunction
(page 128)

Quick fix

RICE

Thomas stretch

RICE

stretches &
massage

back
exercises &
nerve stretches

Hamstring strains and tears

The hamstrings tend to be rather neglected by runners, in terms of strengthening and stretching, although they are a very important muscle, acting as both a hip extensor and knee flexor in the running gait. It's when we ask them for extra power and speed, such as in a sprint finish or acceleration during interval training, that they are most vulnerable to acute tears. But they can also become stressed by chronic overload.

Acute tears

You will know if you have torn your hamstring by the sudden pain in the back of the thigh. It's the classic picture of a runner collapsing, clutching the leg. You'll have to stop immediately and seek help.

What to do
Follow the RICE protocol (see page 113) immediately. Rest the leg for 48 hours, and then start gentle stretching. Once the leg can be straightened almost fully when sitting, you can start jogging. Follow the hamstring rehabilitation program below to ensure the muscle doesn't "go" again. This is essential, as the biggest predictor of a hamstring strain is a previous one. Even if you feel able to run again after a matter of days, take the injury seriously and rehabilitate it properly.

Hamstring rehabilitation program
Start this program when you are pain-free and not limping. Find a suitable area of flat, even grass – a soccer field is good, as you can use the length of the field as a guide to the distance needed. Split the field into three sections.

Jog a mile to warm up. Then, from the "starting" line, gradually build up your pace to the first line, then hold this pace for the mid-section of the field, and finally, use the last third to slow down. Repeat this five times and do three sets, finishing with a mile-long jog to cool-down. Gradually increase the speed of the acceleration on each session until you feel you are running at full speed without any reaction. Try to do this three times a week for about three weeks, interspersing it with steady running sessions. Then you can confidently reintroduce all aspects of speed work into your training.

Chronic strains

Chronic hamstring strains are more common than acute tears in distance runners and occur when the muscle becomes overloaded. The muscle will be tight and painful when stretched and upon resisted action, such as when pulling the heel to the buttocks. There will be local pain and spasm over the tender site, and pain when running. If the strain is mild, this pain will ease off during running but tighten up again afterward.

Hamstring strains often occur as a result of poor gluteal recruitment, forcing the hamstring into a dual role of stabilizing the pelvis and providing power to extend the leg. Poor gluteal activity, in turn, is often caused by overpronation – when the leg turns in, the gluteals are put in an inefficient position and can't function properly. Hamstring overload can also be caused by overtraining or speed work, creating inflammation and micro tears in the muscle fibers or tendon. This tends to be exacerbated when the body is fatigued, as the pelvis tilts forward, putting further strain on the muscles at the back of the leg.

The hamstrings can become overloaded anywhere, but the biceps femoris, the biggest of the hamstring group, is the most common place, because it is a two-joint muscle and thus has to work harder and through a greater range. Problems can occur at either end – runners get a lot of chronic hamstring "origin" pain: in other words, pain where it attaches to the "sit" bone. This can cause pain not only when you are running, but also when driving and sitting.

Tendonitis can also occur at the lower end, in the tendons that run alongside the knee joint, often as a result of faulty biomechanics causing more twisting at the knee. All these problems are treated the same way, although the tendons may be slower to heal because they have a lower blood supply.

The sciatic nerve runs down the middle of the hamstrings and, if it becomes tethered in the spine, can cause tightness, micro tears and inflammation within the muscle. This will need treating locally, but the underlying cause in the spine will need addressing, too.

What to do
Continue to run only if it doesn't hurt to do so during or after your run. Even then, reduce your mileage and eliminate speed work while you allow the muscle to settle. If it does cause pain to run, take a few days rest and follow the advice below. Start by icing the painful area and take anti-inflammatories (but not in the case of an acute tear).

Massage through the tight part of the muscle to release any tension and improve blood flow. Mobilize the lower back using the exercises on pages 122–123. Regularly stretch the muscles, using the exercise on page 37. The hamstring is a two-joint muscle, with medial and lateral components, so rotate the leg both inward and outward to stretch effectively. Also mobilize the sciatic nerve, which can easily become tethered. The slump (page 40) is the most effective way of doing this.

To aid rehabilitation and prevent a recurrence of the problem, it is important to strengthen the hamstrings. You can use a hamstring-curl machine, or stand or lie face-down and kick the heels toward the bottom, progressing by adding a weight to the ankle. Repeat sets of 20 until the muscle starts to feel tired. Make sure the glutes and core are

functioning properly, too. Revisit the core exercises on pages 74–81, especially bridging.

Referred pain
Pain can be referred to the thigh from the spine if there is a minor disc bulge, a condition that is prevalent both among the general population and in runners. This causes an irritation of the sciatic nerve and referred pain into the hamstring region and below. You can also get pins and needles and numbness in the leg. There will be a vague ache and a hard-to-pinpoint pain.

What to do
Mobilize the lower back through its full range using the exercises on pages 122–123 to get rid of any impingement in the spinal joints. Keep the sciatic nerve free from adhesions by doing the mobilizations on pages 40–41, and ensure the spine is well supported by maintaining a strong core (pages 74–81).

Hamstring tendinopathy
This is simply an inflammation of the hamstring tendon, or the bursa underneath it, where it originates from the sitting bone, the ischial tuberosity. It is a classic overuse injury, resulting primarily from short, weak hamstrings. The hamstrings can also overwork if the glutes are not firing correctly.

You'll feel pain locally – very much at the top of the hamstring muscles – and it will probably occur both when running and sitting, and also during stretching and resistance work (such as pulling the heel to the buttock against resistance). Hamstring tendinopathy is often associated with unaccustomed or excessive speed work and track sessions.

What to do
The first port of call is to reduce inflammation with rest, ice and anti-inflammatories.

Start stretching the hamstrings and hip flexors (see page 37), and do the prone kicks on page 28. Put a weight around the ankle and do some standing heel lifts (start with three sets of 20 and gradually increase the speed) and include some glute exercises, such as the bridge (page 76) and lunges (page 88). The hamstring rehabilitation program on page 132 is a good way of gradually loading the tendon.

If work on the actual tendon – such as ultrasound and massage – has no effect on your condition, it's likely that the inflammation lies within the bursa underneath. This may respond to a local anti-inflammatory injection, so see your sports-medicine professional for advice.

Femoral stress fracture
A stress fracture of the femur can result from excessive forces exerted over a period of time. Bone, which is continuously remodeling (replacing itself), doesn't have a chance to produce as much as is being absorbed by the continual stresses placed upon it, leaving a weakened area. This is most commonly seen in young female amenorrheic athletes, but other runners, particularly those who increase their training volume too much or too quickly, are not immune.

Biomechanical faults, particularly turning-in of the hipbone and overpronation, can also make you more

vulnerable. A stress fracture will present as a deep pain in the thigh that you will be unable to pinpoint. Alarm bells should ring if there is pain on hopping, or if the pain gets worse with running and aches at rest. You may also suffer pain at night.

What to do
Rest immediately. The sooner you rest, the sooner the problem will settle.

Get your biomechanics checked. Review your training: has there been a sudden increase in mileage? Also ensure that you have sufficient calcium in your diet.

Quadriceps strain
A quadriceps strain isn't as common in runners as a hamstring strain, but it can and does happen. The rectus femoris is the most likely part of the muscle group to be affected as, like the biceps femoris, it is a two-joint muscle and therefore more vulnerable to stress.

The cause, as in hamstring strains, can be spinal or local, again from overload (through excessive training or insufficient muscle strength) or poor biomechanics.

Tightness in the upper lumbar facet joints of the lower back puts a lot of irritation on the femoral nerve (the one supplying the quads). If this is irritated, it can cause tightness and pain in the muscle and sometimes local inflammation. The quads will be tight and painful to stretch, and there will be a local area of pain. You may get some pain on running, which will ease off as you progress, but stiffen up afterward.

What to do
Ice the local area and use anti-inflammatories. Try some local massage to the tight area. Stretch the quadriceps muscles religiously, using the Thomas stretch (see page 39), and mobilize the femoral nerve (see page 41). Mobilize the lower back with the exercises on pages 122–123.

SARAH'S CASEBOOK

The last two stress fractures that I saw were in males who had increased their mileage too quickly. One had pain on running, but more intense pain when hopping and playing tennis after running. The other had a diffuse pain that couldn't be located, but also had pain on hopping. Both were caught early and responded well to three weeks rest followed by gradual loading.

Adductor tendinopathy

The adductor complex is a set of five muscles along the inside of the thigh. Each has its own role, depending on the position of the leg, in either flexing or extending the hip. The adductors also work hard to stabilize the pelvis while running. This multitasking role makes them vulnerable to damage and overload, resulting in inflammation of the common tendon of origin, adductor tendinopathy. There will be pain on the inside of the thigh up to the pubic bone, and pain on squeezing the knees together. If you get pins and needles, the nerve supplying the groin area may be trapped and inflamed. This area is very pain-sensitive, so adductor tendinopathy can be quite debilitating. What's more, the blood supply around the tendon area is poor, so healing is slow.

The main risk factor for adductor tendinopathy is excessive tightness of the muscles. When the adductors are short and tight, they pull on the pelvis when you increase your running speed, causing it to become unstable and irritating the tendon. The adductors can also be overloaded from running on soft, uneven ground if your feet keep slipping.

What to do
Ice and anti-inflammatories will help, but icing this area is only for the brave! Don't use drugs to mask the pain and run through – if it hurts to run, rest; if it doesn't, at least cut out speed work temporarily. Start stretching the area as soon as possible. Improve hip stability by doing the "hip hitching" exercise on page 18. The bridge (page 76) is another good exercise for stabilizing the pelvis. Do some standing adductor exercises using a resistance tube: tie one end to a secure structure, and then, with the band over one ankle, pull the leg toward and slightly across the other. Also try to mobilize the nerve, using the modified Thomas exercise on page 41. Once you are back running, ensure that adductor stretches are part of your warm-up.

The knee
Knee injuries are among the most common in runners, especially chronic or "overuse" problems. Many of these are vague and non-specific – and often a result of tightness in surrounding structures such as the iliotibial band, quadriceps, hamstrings and connective tissues – so it's important to look at the whole picture, and not solely at the knee.

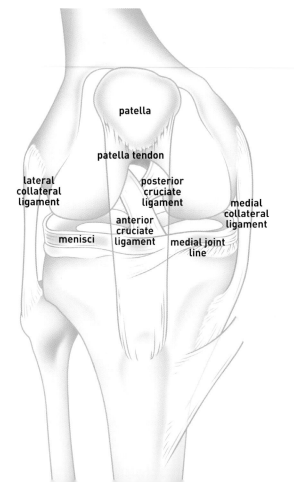

The **patella** (kneecap) sits at the front of the knee, attached to the quadriceps muscles above and the tibia below via the patella tendon. The **patella tendon** is very strong, transmitting all the forces from knee extension.

Four ligaments provide support and stability to the knee joint: the **anterior cruciate**, **posterior cruciate** and the **medial** and **lateral collateral**. Injuries to these ligaments aren't common in running – other than from falls or collisions.

The **menisci** are moon-shaped structures that act as the shock absorbers for the knee.

The **medial joint line** is a common site for medial meniscal pain, as it's an area where three structures meet: the medial meniscus, the medial collateral ligament and the knee capsule itself.

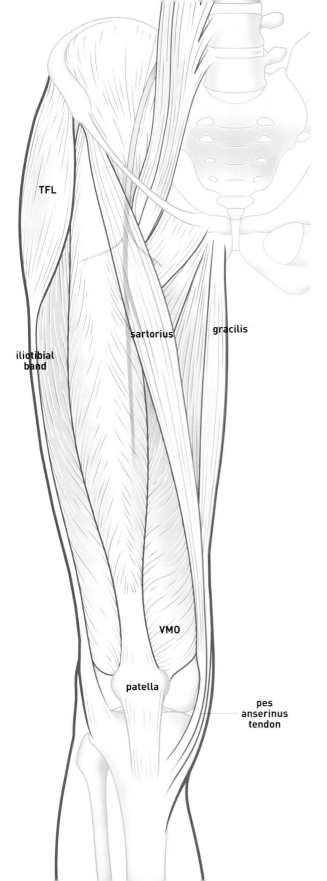

TFL

sartorius

gracilis

iliotibial
band

VMO

patella

pes
anserinus
tendon

A long, fibrous band of tissue called the **iliotibial band (ITB)** extends all the way from the hip to below the knee. Overactivity of the hip flexors, especially the **tensor fasciae latae (TFL)**, can cause it to tighten, so that during running it "flicks" over the side of the knee either at the top outside edge (the femoral condyle) or the lower outside edge of the knee (Gerdy's tubercle).

The lowest fibers of the vastus medialis muscle are at an oblique angle, causing many physical therapists to distinguish it as a separate muscle – the **vastus medialis obliquus (VMO)**. It has an important role in preventing the patella "drifting" laterally.

Three muscles – the **sartorius**, **gracilis** and **semitendinosus** (one of the hamstring group, see page 130) – converge at the inside of the knee to form the **pes anserinus tendon**. If the adductors and medial hamstrings are tight, tendonitis can occur here.

knee pain symptoms map (see note on page 115)

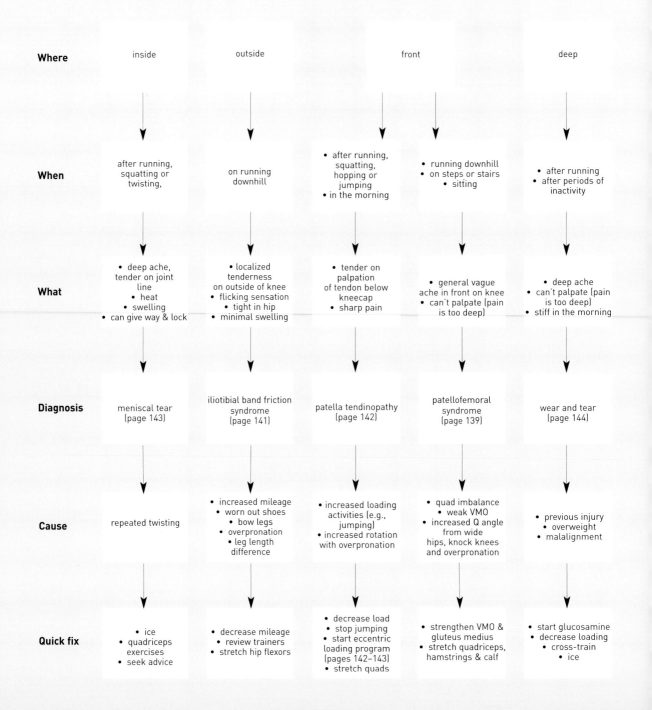

	inside	outside	front		deep
Where	inside	outside	front		deep
When	after running, squatting or twisting,	on running downhill	• after running, squatting, hopping or jumping • in the morning	• running downhill • on steps or stairs • sitting	• after running • after periods of inactivity
What	• deep ache, tender on joint line • heat • swelling • can give way & lock	• localized tenderness on outside of knee • flicking sensation • tight in hip • minimal swelling	• tender on palpation of tendon below kneecap • sharp pain	• general vague ache in front on knee • can't palpate (pain is too deep)	• deep ache • can't palpate (pain is too deep) • stiff in the morning
Diagnosis	meniscal tear (page 143)	iliotibial band friction syndrome (page 141)	patella tendinopathy (page 142)	patellofemoral syndrome (page 139)	wear and tear (page 144)
Cause	repeated twisting	• increased mileage • worn out shoes • bow legs • overpronation • leg length difference	• increased loading activities (e.g., jumping) • increased rotation with overpronation	• quad imbalance • weak VMO • increased Q angle from wide hips, knock knees and overpronation	• previous injury • overweight • malalignment
Quick fix	• ice • quadriceps exercises • seek advice	• decrease mileage • review trainers • stretch hip flexors	• decrease load • stop jumping • start eccentric loading program (pages 142–143) • stretch quads	• strengthen VMO & gluteus medius • stretch quadriceps, hamstrings & calf	• start glucosamine • decrease loading • cross-train • ice

Runner's knee (anterior knee pain)

One of the most common injury problems runners face is patellofemoral pain syndrome (PFPS), sometimes known as anterior knee pain. This is a classic case of a chronic injury, which creeps up on you quite gradually in the form of a vague, hard-to-put-your-finger-on pain around the front of the knee. It's usually made worse by going downstairs and is often called "theater knee" as prolonged sitting can cause it to ache or throb as a result of increased pressure on the subchondral bone, which is the deep layer of bone underneath the articular cartilage. Unlike articular cartilage, the subchondral bone has a lot of nerve endings, so it's very pain-sensitive.

What causes PFPS? Well, the kneecap sits in a groove on the femur and runs up and down this groove – like a train on tracks – as the leg bends and straightens. But if any of the structures around the knee are pulling incorrectly, or exerting too much or too little force, the patella can be pulled out of line so that it no longer runs smoothly in its groove.

This maltracking can increase loading on the joint surfaces. The two areas most commonly affected are the femoral trochlea, where the patella sits, and the medial facet, on the inside edge of the patella, where it is pulled across and "bangs" into the side of the groove of the femur. The other structures affected by maltracking are the synovium (an extremely sensitive structure that provides the lining of the joint), the lateral retinaculum (the thickened part of the fibrous capsule of the knee), the muscles attached to the patella and the nerves around the front of the knee. All these need to be investigated to see which is causing the symptoms – it could be a combination.

So, maltracking causes PFPS, but what causes the maltracking? The most common cause is an imbalance in the strength of the muscles on the inside and outside of the thigh. The strength ratio between the outermost quad, the vastus lateralis, and the innermost one, the vastus medialis, should be 1:1, but often in cases of PFPS the medialis is weaker, allowing the kneecap to drift to the side (laterally) as the quadriceps contract. What's more, any inflammation or swelling in the knee causes the very sensitive vastus medialis obliquus (VMO) muscle to "switch off," so just when it's needed to prevent the kneecap drifting, it stops working altogether.

Another important muscle to consider is actually nowhere near the knee. The gluteus medius in the bottom works in tandem with the VMO to keep the leg aligned. If the knee rolls in, the VMO and gluteus medius are not in an efficient position to work, so the tensor fasciae latae (TFL), an abductor, takes over. If the TFL is working overtime, it can pull on the iliotibial band (ITB) too, increasing the lateral pull on the kneecap. The ITB connects to the outside border of the patella via a band of tissue. The lateral pull on the kneecap can cause this tissue itself to become sore and inflamed.

What to do

Anti-inflammatories and ice help to settle chronic conditions like runner's knee, but don't use them to mask the pain and run through the injury: use them to settle the inflammation so that you can begin rehabilitation. Taping is another option – research from Australia suggests it is an effective strategy for dealing with patellofemoral pain. Taping can physically change the position of the patella, unloading it and allowing the area to settle down. You should also assess your trainers, ensuring they are the right type for your foot shape and are in good condition.

To prevent a recurrence of the condition, you need to find out what is causing your knees to roll in. It can be a result of overpronation at the foot, an inward rotation of the hips, or tight calf muscles. If the gluteus medius muscle is weak, the leg will internally rotate more, especially when you are tired. Get a physical therapist or other sports-medicine expert to assess your running technique, muscle strength and flexibility – particularly in the quadriceps, calves and hip flexors. Tight quadriceps can increase the loading of the patella, as the shorter they are, the greater their pull over the knee. Once you get back to training, avoid running down steep hills for a while.

Exercises for runner's knee

These exercises work the muscles that stabilize the knee joint. They can be done twice daily, as they are not so much strength exercises as recruitment practice – the frequency helps the muscle "remember" what to do. In addition to the exercises shown here, you could also try the Thomas stretch (see page 39) and the clam (page 75, repeat 10 times).

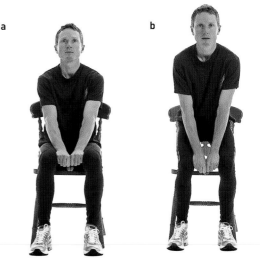

a   b

1 Sitting squat
Sit toward the front of a chair and put your fists between your knees **(a)**. Squeeze tight and hold for 10 seconds. Repeat 10 times.

To progress, squeeze and then stand up **(b)**.

2 Wall dip
Standing by a wall, rest the "good" leg against the wall or a solid surface about hip height, so you are standing on the "bad" leg. Bend the knee of the "bad" leg 30 degrees and try to turn the knee outward. Hold for 20 seconds. Repeat five times.

3 Leg extension

Sit on a chair, extend the leg to approximately 30 degrees **(a)** and then fully straighten **(b)**. Raise and lower the leg through this 30-degree range. Repeat 20 times.

a

b

PRACTICE MAKES PERFECT

It has been found that people in China hardly suffer runner's knee at all. This may be due to the fact that they spend a lot of time sitting cross-legged, meaning the medial facet or groove on the patella is much more used to contact and loading, and is less soft.

Iliotibial band friction syndrome

The iliotibial band (ITB) is a thickening of the fascia that runs down the outside of the leg. It attaches to the tensor fasciae latae (TFL) at the front of the hip and to part of the gluteus maximus at the back of the hip. It then extends down to the outside edge of the tibia and to the head of the fibula, as well as attaching to the patella via the lateral retinaculum. ITB friction syndrome is localized pain on the outside of the knee when the leg is bent. The pain is usually felt either around the femoral condyle at the top outside edge of the knee or Gerdy's tubercle on the outside edge of the tibia at the bottom outside edge of the knee. Sometimes a "flicking" sensation is felt as the ITB passes over the outer edge of the thigh bone. ITB pain is often worse when going up and down stairs and during downhill running.

ITB pain can be caused by biomechanical alignment problems, such as bow legs, overpronation or a leg length difference, all of which result in increased load on the outside of the leg. But it can also be due to training errors. Running on the slant of the road, or on a track, are other possible causes, as they load one leg more than the other. Running when fatigued can also cause ITB friction syndrome, as the legs tend to turn in, increasing lateral loading of the knee. Fatigue also contributes to hip drop, as the tired hip stabilizers are unable to keep the pelvis level during running.

What to do

Ice can help settle the inflammation in the painful area, as can anti-inflammatories – but don't use them to mask the pain and run. Self-massage over the ITB, especially the lower fibers nearer the knee, can help. The best position is lying on your side with the knees bent and the ITB relaxed. A tennis ball can work well as a massage tool, or, if you can bear it, try rolling the outside of the painful leg over a foam roller (obtainable from your physical therapist).

SARAH'S CASEBOOK

Pain isn't always caused by something in the immediate area. ITB friction syndrome can result from tightness of the lower back, causing the femoral nerve to tighten the lateral structures of the leg. I have had a lot of success, even on stubborn ITB problems, with treatment to the spine, so don't be afraid to ask your physical therapist.

Strengthen the hip abductors to prevent the pelvis tilting during running. If the glutes are weak, the TFL muscle overworks, pulling on the top end of the ITB and causing tightness. The clam and the bridge (see pages 75–76) are good exercises to strengthen the appropriate muscles. Perform the cross-leg stretch below daily.

Cross-leg stretch
Stand near a wall with one leg resting behind the other and the front knee bent, then lean into the wall toward the resting leg until you feel a stretch on the outside of that thigh; hold for 30 seconds and repeat two or three times per leg.

If you are pain free, it's fine to run, but only as far as you can without pain setting in. If you can't run at all without pain, focus on stretching and strengthening for a couple of weeks. If, after that, the condition persists, seek advice from a sports-injury expert.

Patella tendonitis/tendinosis

The patella tendon attaches the kneecap to the tibia and the quadriceps muscle. Tendinosis is degeneration of the tendon, while tendonitis is inflammation. The pain is usually at the bottom of the kneecap, where it attaches to the tendon, and there is sometimes associated inflammation of the fat pad that sits under the tendon.

There are two main causes of patella tendonitis. First, there may be excessive eccentric overload of the quadriceps (in other words, overload while the muscles are lengthening), which causes breakdown of the tendon and an inflammatory response. Second, microtrauma (tiny amounts of damage to the tendon fibers) may occur as a result of repeated strain on the tendon due to biomechanical misalignments, such as overpronation, turning-in of the hips or knees, or excessive tightness in the quadriceps muscles. The pain can usually be felt on palpation (touching the sore area) and is worse on squatting and using stairs.

What to do

Tendon problems should be rested early. They can take three to six months to recover. If you ignore the early signs of tendonitis, it will quickly become tendinosis. A tendon injury is graded from 1 to 4: 1 being pain after exercise and 4 being pain on general daily activities. An ignored stage one problem will quickly progress to a stubborn stage 4.

Ice and anti-inflammatories will help during the rest period, as will stretching the quadriceps, hamstrings and calf muscles. Have your gait checked out for any abnormalities and get your trainers assessed, too. As

Decline squats
Stand facing down a slope
(the steeple jump pit at an
athletics track is perfect).
Squat down to about 90
degrees, keeping your back
straight **(a)**. Aim for three
sets of 20 repeats.

Progress, when you can, to
doing this on one leg **(b)**.

a   b

soon as possible, start the decline squats above. These
have been clinically proven to be the most effective
way of rehabilitating the tendon. It is normal to have
some pain during and after this exercise initially.

Don't even think about trying to run until there is no
pain on palpation, or on one-leg squats, and when
you do resume training, make sure you build up your
mileage very gradually. You can still use ice after
exercise, but not before, as this will limit blood supply
to the tendon.

SARAH'S CASEBOOK

A new technique called sclerosing therapy is being used
to treat tendon injuries. It has been shown that extra
blood vessels develop as a result of the body's attempt
to heal the tendonitis – but this actually increases the
inflammatory response and causes pain. The sclerosing
agents destroy these extra vessels. You need to see a
sports medicine specialist for this treatment.

Cartilage problems
Two small, crescent-shaped cartilages called menisci
sit inside the joint between the femur and tibia and
absorb shock. They can get damaged or torn by
twisting, either in the case of an acute injury (such
as a fall) or by repeated low-level twists. There is
normally swelling in the joint and tenderness over the
joint line between the femur and tibia. It is easier to
feel this on the inside of the knee with the knee bent.
There is a usually a "clicking" in the knee and pain
upon squatting, and the knee may lock or give way.

What to do
Get suspected meniscal problems assessed, as the
constant inflammatory presence in the joint and the
incorrect transference of forces can be a risk factor
for early osteoarthritis. The first treatment for a
meniscal tear may be a local anti-inflammatory, via
either injection therapy or electrotherapy. Or you may
be offered an arthroscopy, the "keyhole" surgery that
is used to trim the worn bits of cartilage that are
catching. This is normally performed in a day and
rehabilitation takes only a matter of weeks.

Wear and tear

Degenerative changes in the joint surfaces are classed as "wear and tear" in the joint, or osteoarthritis (OA). This is where the articular cartilage – the cartilage that coats the bone endings – becomes worn and damaged, leading to a bumpy, uneven joint surface. You can often feel thickening around the joint line where extra bone has laid down in the process. The joint may be hot and inflamed and will stiffen up with inactivity, especially first thing in the morning. Sufferers often feel a deep, but non-specific ache in the joint.

It hasn't been proved that running causes this problem – some very recent research published in the journal *Arthritis Care and Research* concluded, after looking at over 1000 people, that recreational running did not increase the risk of OA. However, there are three risk factors that should be taken into consideration: previous injury to that joint, misalignment and being overweight. In all three, the likelihood of OA in the knee is higher for runners.

There is a new therapy for OA, in which hyaluronic acid is injected into the joint to provide more lubrication. You need to be referred to a sports medicine specialist for this treatment. Supplementation with glucosamine sulphate and chondroitin has also shown some promising results in trials.

Keeping the quadriceps muscles strong is another important step to take. Consider incorporating some non-impact cross-training into your regimen to decrease overall load on the joint (see chapter 8 for some ideas).

Pes anserinus tendonitis/bursitis

Problems with this strangely named tendon are not as common as some of the aforementioned injuries, but they can and do occur, generally as a result of the muscles on the inside of the legs being tight. The pes anserinus tendon runs along the inside of the knee and is an amalgamation of the three tendons of the sartorius, gracilis and semitendinosus muscles. Tendonitis occurs when the tension on the area is too great, causing inflammation of the tendon and the underlying bursae. There can be "crepitus," a grating sensation as the knee moves in the tendon, which you will feel along the inside of the knee down to the top of the tibia.

What to do

Self-massage and ice can help to start with, but most cases will respond successfully to stretching of the adductors and inner hamstrings. Don't forget that there are long and short adductors, so do your inner-thigh stretches with legs both straight and bent. To stretch the inner hamstrings, use your normal hamstring stretch but turn the foot inward to focus on the hamstrings on the inner side of the thigh. Inflammation of the bursae underlying the tendon is sometimes resolved with a local anti-inflammatory injection.

Twists and falls

In a twisting injury or fall it is possible to damage any of the knee's structures. Remember RICE (see page 113) and get an immediate diagnosis. The most common ligaments to suffer damage in a twisting injury are the medial collateral ligament (MCL) and the anterior cruciate ligament (ACL). Damage to the medial meniscus is also common in twisting injuries. If there is an immediate swelling, there will be blood in the joint, which is indicative of structural damage. This is called a hemarthrosis and a trip to the ER is normally required. If the swelling is gradual and takes longer than 24 hours to develop, it may be less serious – but you should still get a professional diagnosis.

Knee strengthening and rehabilitation

It is vital to strengthen the knee and its surrounding structures following any knee-related injury. The following program offers a progressive return to normal strength. Try three sets of 20 reps of each exercise on each leg where applicable (not just on the injured leg). Once hopping is pain-free, you can start running again.

1 Bridge

Lie on your back with knees bent and arms folded across your chest. Slowly curl the spine up off the floor, starting at the tailbone, until the body forms a straight line from the shoulders to the knees. Hold for 5 seconds, building up to10 seconds. Repeat 10 times.

2 Static squat with the back against a wall

Start with the back resting against a wall and slowly bend the knees to just before 90 degrees, then try to hold for 10 seconds.

3 Static squat with one leg supported by a wall

Rest one leg against the wall and bend the other knee to 30 degrees and try to turn the knee outward. Hold for 10 seconds.

4 Squat on both legs without support
Start by standing with feet shoulder width apart and bend the knees, keeping the back straight. Hold for 10 seconds.

5 Squat on one leg without support
Stand on one leg and bend the supporting knee to approximately 45 degrees.

6 Repeat the two-leg squat, holding either dumbbells or wearing a weighted jacket **(not shown)**.

7 Step-up
Stand in front of a step and step up with one leg, then back down with the other.

8 Step-down
Stand on a step and step down forward, then step up backward with the other leg.

9 Step-up sideways
Stand sideways on a step
and step up and down the
same side.

10 Hop
Stand on one leg and hop
into the air, landing on the
same leg.

The lower leg

The area below the knee and above the foot is an injury hotspot for runners, with problems like shin splints, calf strains and Achilles tendonitis wreaking havoc and misery.

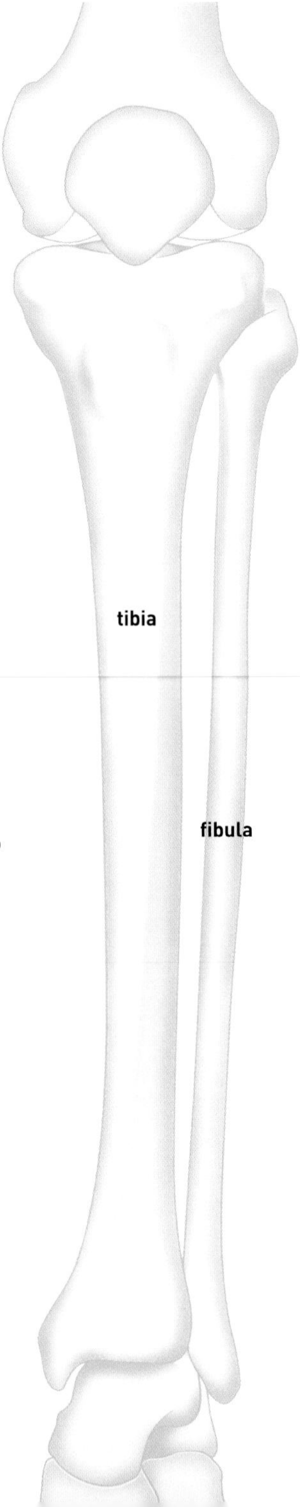

The lower limb contains two bones, the **tibia** and **fibula**. The tibia is the main weight-bearing bone.

tibia

fibula

The small muscles on the front of the leg are the **tibialis anterior**, **extensor digitorum longus** and **extensor hallucis longus** – all work to lift the foot and toes. If you have problems lifting your foot, the nerve could be trapped. This is commonly known as a "dropped" foot, and you'll hear a "slapping" gait as you walk.

The muscles on the outside of the leg, the **peronei**, attach to the fibula, and the tendons run under the ankle bone. These are necessary for balance and proprioception.

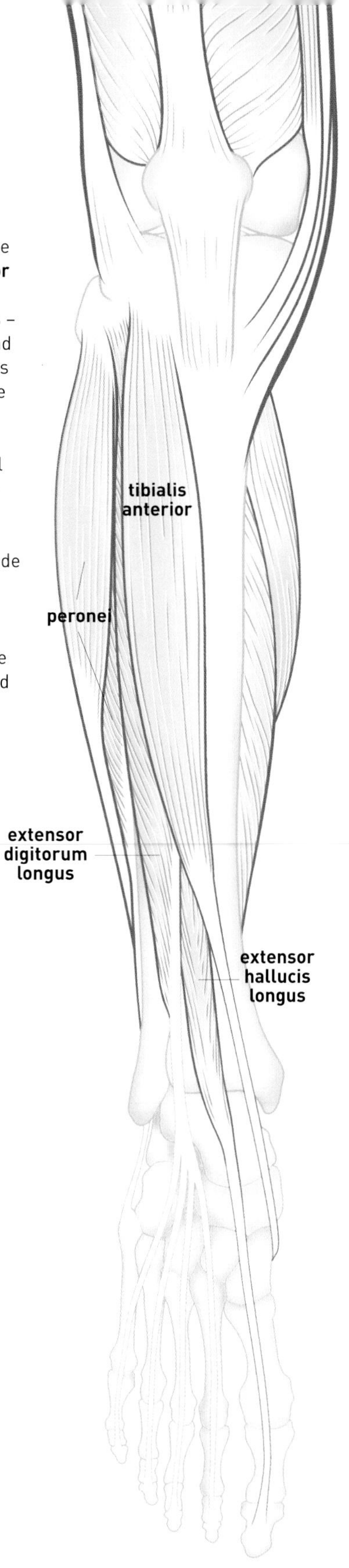

tibialis anterior

peronei

extensor digitorum longus

extensor hallucis longus

The back of the lower leg has three layers of muscle, the **gastrocnemius** (which attaches above the knee), the **soleus** (which attaches below the knee) and the **deep flexors** of the foot.

Both the calf muscles (the gastrocnemius and soleus) attach to the **Achilles tendon**, which inserts at the back of the heel bone. The strongest tendon in the body, it is encased in a sheath, which contains most of its blood supply.

The tendon is separated from the top part of the heel bone by a bursa (fluid-filled sac) that eases friction.

The gastrocnemius provides the propelling force in running – the soleus is the stabilizer.

The gastrocnemius crosses over three joints – the knee, the ankle and the subtalar joint. This means that tension in structures affecting these joints have a direct effect on the Achilles.

The **plantaris** is a small, often overlooked muscle that runs alongside the main calf muscles, next to the Achilles tendon.

The deep layer of muscles includes the **flexor digitorum longus**, which bends the toes, and the **tibialis posterior**, which lifts the arch. Both of these muscles attach to the inside of the tibia and are crucial to the control of the foot during running.

The medial side of the tibia, where the deep flexors attach, is a common site for bone stress.

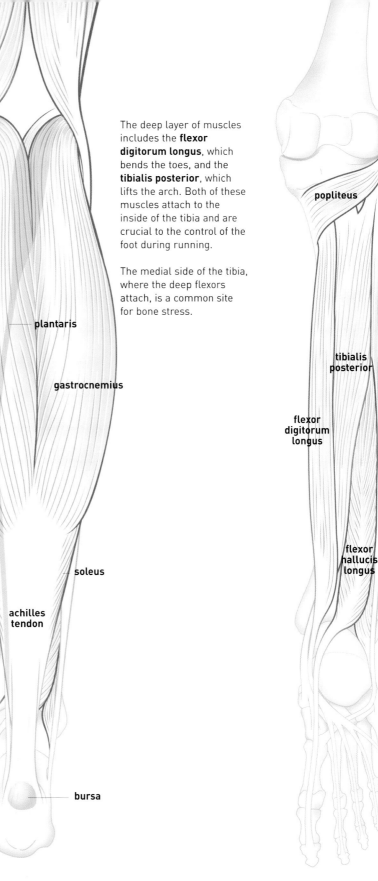

plantaris

gastrocnemius

soleus

achilles tendon

bursa

popliteus

tibialis posterior

flexor digitorum longus

flexor hallucis longus

lower leg pain symptoms map (see note on page 115)

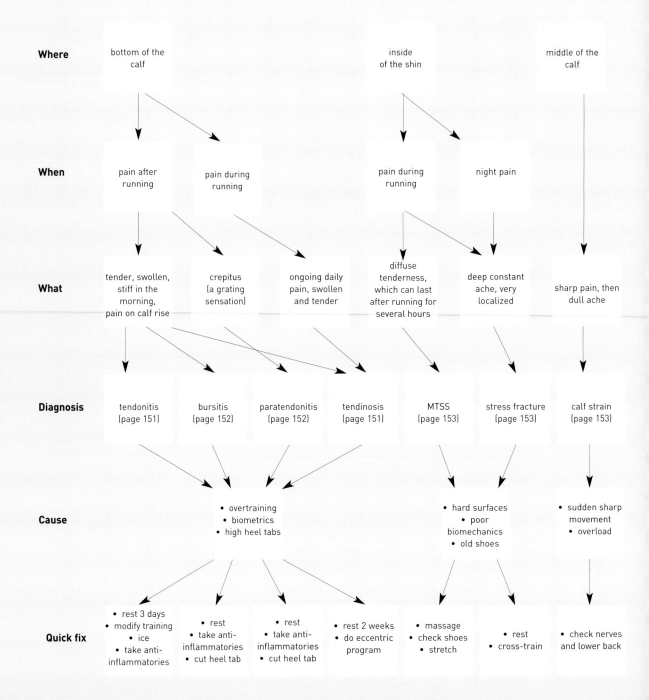

Where

bottom of the calf

inside of the shin

middle of the calf

When

pain after running

pain during running

pain during running

night pain

What

tender, swollen, stiff in the morning, pain on calf rise

crepitus (a grating sensation)

ongoing daily pain, swollen and tender

diffuse tenderness, which can last after running for several hours

deep constant ache, very localized

sharp pain, then dull ache

Diagnosis

tendonitis (page 151)

bursitis (page 152)

paratendonitis (page 152)

tendinosis (page 151)

MTSS (page 153)

stress fracture (page 153)

calf strain (page 153)

Cause

- overtraining
- biometrics
- high heel tabs

- hard surfaces
- poor biomechanics
- old shoes

- sudden sharp movement
- overload

Quick fix

- rest 3 days
- modify training
- ice
- take anti-inflammatories

- rest
- take anti-inflammatories
- cut heel tab

- rest
- take anti-inflammatories
- cut heel tab

- rest 2 weeks
- do eccentric program

- massage
- check shoes
- stretch

- rest
- cross-train

- check nerves and lower back

Achilles problems

The Achilles is one of the most common problem areas for runners, but the biggest cause of such problems is ignoring the first signs of pain during and after running (so do so at your peril!). There are five main types of Achilles injury.

Achilles tendonitis

This is inflammation of the tendon, which, if caught early enough and addressed, will settle quite easily. It can be caused by tight calf muscles, stiffness in the foot and ankle, or simply by running too much or increasing training too quickly. Biomechanical problems, such as overpronation, can also be a factor. Tendonitis is characterized by early morning stiffness, which you will be able to run off initially.

What to do

If the pain is only mild and occasional, modify your training by cutting out hills and speed work. Ice the area after running and try the exercises later in this chapter. If the pain is more severe and persistent, stop running while you address the problem. You may want to take anti-inflammatories. Massage to the calf muscle can also help (but avoid massage directly over the tendon).

Assess your trainers. Do they have a high heel tab, which could be rubbing the tendon? Putting some small heel raises in your trainers will offload the tendon slightly.

Do the calf stretch on page 38 and the straight-leg raise for nerve mobilization on page 41. If none of the above helps, seek advice from a physical therapist or other sports-medicine expert.

Achilles tendinosis

While tendonitis is inflammation, tendinosis is actual degeneration of the tendon – and it can be the result of

> **SARAH'S CASEBOOK**
>
> The last two Achilles problems I treated have both been due to spinal tension loading the calf and Achilles complex. They have both settled completely with spinal treatment, nerve mobilizations and minimal local treatment. If your Achilles isn't settling from the strategies outlined here, don't be afraid to ask your therapist to look at your back.

ignored or poorly rehabilitated tendonitis. The tendon becomes thicker, blood supply is reduced and sometimes white plaques (that look like toothpaste) and cysts form along and inside the tendon, causing pain not just during running but during daily activities, too. The decreased blood supply stops the tendon healing, creating a vicious circle that is tricky to break.

What to do

All of the advice for Achilles tendonitis applies to tendinosis, too, although anti-inflammatories are not so necessary. Alternating ice with heat can help improve local blood flow to the tendon. Try dunking your lower leg into a bucket filled with iced water alternated with one filled with hot water.

There's one crucial additional thing to do for tendinosis: the eccentric calf exercise, as described on the next page. Australian research has shown that this is the only way to get tendons to regenerate or heal, but even then it can be a long process, taking three to six months. This is where your cross-training will really come into play.

It is worth looking into sclerosing injections (see "Sarah's casebook" on page 143) if your Achilles problem is particularly resistant to treatment.

Eccentric calf exercise

Stand on a step with the ball of the foot and toes on the edge, the heels dropped below **(a)**. Rise up onto your toes **(b)**, then drop down below the level of the step. Start with two legs and, as pain and strength allow, progress to one leg. You should be able to do three sets of 20 repetitions on a single leg before running recommences and three sets of 40 single-leg repetitions before speed work resumes.

Expect to have some delayed onset muscle soreness (DOMS) initially after doing these exercises.

a   b

Achilles paratenonitis

Like all tendons, the Achilles is encased in a sheath, and paratenonitis occurs when the sheath becomes inflamed. With this condition, you'll often feel a "creaking" along the back of the lower leg as you bend and extend the foot – this is caused by friction between the sheath and the tendon.

What to do

The possible causes of paratenonitis are the same as for tendonitis, though a chafing heel tab on your trainers is often the culprit. If you think this may be the problem, cut off the heel tab. Treat as for tendonitis – with ice, modified training and calf stretching. If the condition doesn't settle, seek advice.

Achilles bursitis

Achilles bursitis presents itself as pain in front of the tendon, which you'll feel when you point the foot. The fluid-filled bursa sits between the tendon and the back of the heel to prevent friction, so when it is inflamed and you point the foot, it gets squashed, causing pain.

What to do

Once again, the causes and treatment strategies are the same as for Achilles tendon problems. If none of these helps to settle the problem, a local anti-inflammatory injection into the bursa may help.

Ruptured Achilles

The Achilles tendon can rupture when the force it is subjected to exceeds its strength. A complete or partial rupture needs surgery to fix it and then 12 weeks in a cast. This is one condition that is more common with increasing age because of the decrease in blood supply to the tendon. If you rupture your Achilles, you will feel as if you have been shot in the leg and will have no power to rise onto your toes. Go straight to the ER.

> **SARAH'S CASEBOOK**
>
> An anti-inflammatory cortisone injection might sound like the perfect way to settle an irritated Achilles, but research has shown that injections of local steroid into the tendon itself can weaken it and may lead to rupture.

Calf problems

There's no doubting an acute calf tear: it's extremely painful, and you won't be able to continue running. Follow the RICE procedure (page 113) as soon as possible, and after 48 hours start gentle stretching and strengthening. The eccentric calf exercise opposite should help.

Runners often experience tightness in the calf, which isn't due to a tear or strain. The pain can be quite deep and persistent during running, and it often follows faster sessions like track work. This tightness can be caused by overload of the calf muscles (which work harder during faster-paced running) or by tight spinal structures, causing irritation of the sciatic nerve that goes down to the calf. The nerve can become tethered (stuck) and inflamed, leading to either referred calf pain or tightness.

What to do
Stretch all three groups of calf muscle after running (see page 38) and ice any sore areas. Consider getting a sports massage, or massage the area yourself with anti-inflammatory cream – you may find a specific "knot" of tightness, which you can release. It is also worth doing the sciatic nerve mobilizations (pages 40–41) and spinal mobility exercises (pages 122–123).

Shin problems

Although the term "shin splints" is widely used, it doesn't actually refer to a single injury but to a group of conditions affecting the shin that occur as a result of the repetitive nature of running and the high incidence of overpronation.

Medial tibial stress syndrome

Medial tibial stress syndrome (MTSS) is pain and inflammation on the medial border of the tibia, usually felt during and after running. It can be caused by running too much on hard surfaces, overpronation,

a weak tibialis posterior muscle (which lifts the arch of the foot), or tight calf muscles, which cause the foot to pronate further. All the muscles involved in controlling pronation can be affected by MTSS and become sore and inflamed.

MTSS can also affect the fascia (the connective tissue that joins the muscle to the bone) and the periosteum (the outer layer of bone) itself. If the periosteum is inflamed, you'll feel specific tenderness along the edge of the bone.

What to do
Massage the tight muscles along the inside of the shin and the calf before running, and stretch them (see page 38) after warming up. Ice and massage after running will help settle the inflammation – but don't run through pain. A balance of strength on the front and back of the lower leg is important. Strengthen the calf and shin muscles using the exercises at the end of this section. Check your shoes and consider getting gait analysis. Vary the surfaces that you run on, avoiding excessive slant.

If none of the above suggestions help, you will need treatment to release the tight structures around the foot, ankle and calf.

Stress fractures

A stress fracture is caused by repetitive overload of the bone, and while it can happen independently, it can also result from MTSS that hasn't been addressed. The most common site to be affected is along the inside of the tibia, but the lateral side of the fibula can also be affected. The classic symptom of a stress fracture is a very localized area that is tender to touch. If you try to run, pain will increase and won't ease off. There may also be pain at rest and during the night. Never try to run through a stress fracture – it will get worse, and it could fracture completely.

What to do

If you suspect a stress fracture, seek advice. If possible, get an isotope bone scan to confirm the problem. A normal x-ray won't show a stress fracture until healing has started. Rest for four to six weeks until the pain has settled, but be prepared to have to wait up to three months for complete recovery. If you continue to run, you risk being put in a cast, which will make cross-training far more difficult, so be warned.

Make sure your diet contains enough calcium, which aids bone health, and consider having your gait analyzed to prevent future problems. When you return to running, ensure that it's very gradual and on soft surfaces – see chapter 11 for more advice on getting back on track.

Compartment syndrome

The least common calf problem is compartment syndrome, which is when the muscle becomes too tight for its sheath. This is brought on by increased muscle volume as a result of exercise and is often caused by increasing training too quickly. There will be a tight, pressure-like pain on exercise, but no pain when you stop or when the area is touched. It can be associated with pins and needles and weakness, due to compression of the nerves surrounding the muscle.

What to do

Modify your training volume or rest, and use massage and anti-inflammatories. If the pain is severe, surgery to release the pressure may be an option.

Shin strengthening

Resisting lift (above)
Starting position: While sitting, secure a resistance band around both feet, across the instep.

Exercise: Pull the toes of one foot up toward you, against the resistance. Do three sets of 20 on each leg.

Forefoot lift (left)
Starting position: Stand with your back against a wall and feet about 30 cm away.

Exercise: Try to lift the forefeet off the ground, keeping the heels on the ground. Repeat 20 times and try three sets. Once this is easy, increase the speed.

Heel walk (right)
Starting position: Stand on both legs.

Exercise: Try walking on your heels with the toes and forefeet off the ground. Start with a short distance of about 10 m and gradually increase, as you are able.

To progress: Take one foot off the floor and try to hop on one heel. Make sure you do this on soft ground.

Calf rehabilitation

A strengthening program is essential for all calf rehabilitation to allow a successful return to running. Start with the first exercise and progress to the level you can do without pain. Add each new exercise when you are able to do three sets of 20 of the current one pain-free. Before you begin, warm up with some balance exercises, standing on one leg with your eyes closed, or invest in a wobble board (see Resources, page 181).

1 Start with both feet on the floor. Rise up onto your toes, then lower **(left)**.

2 Start with one foot on the floor, holding onto a wall for balance, if required. Rise up onto the toes of that foot, then lower **(right)**.

3 Start with toes on a step as on page 152. Lower the heels below the step, then lift yourself up onto your toes, lower again and repeat **(not shown)**.

4 With one foot on the step and holding the wall for balance if needed, lower the heel below the level of the step, lift up onto your toes and lower again **(left)**.

5 Repeat exercise 3, either holding dumbbells or wearing a weighted jacket. Then repeat again, increasing the speed of the up-and-down movement **(not shown)**.

6 Step up onto the step with one foot and jump into the air. Land on one or both feet, depending on which is more comfortable **(left)**.

The foot and ankle

The foot is a hugely important area for the runner, because it is the initial point of contact with the ground and directs all the forces through the body. If the foot is out of alignment or not functioning properly, a lot can go wrong further up the kinetic chain.

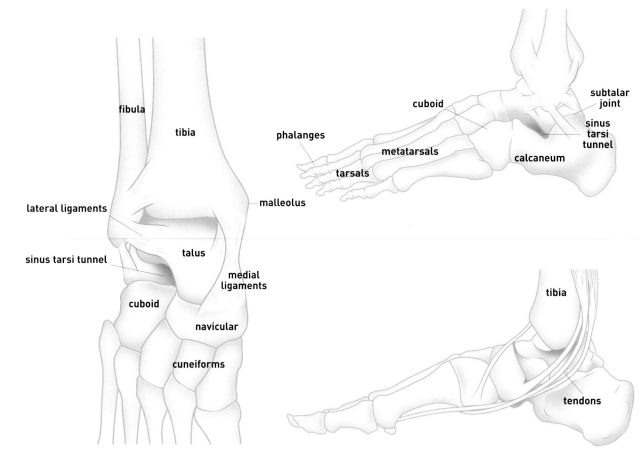

The **ankle joint** is the articulation between the leg and the foot. It is where the **tibia**, **fibula** and **talus** meet. The **malleoli**, the bones on either side of the joint that you can see, form the sides of the ankle joint, which is strengthened on both sides by the **medial** and **lateral ligaments**.

The foot is split into three sections: **rear**, **middle** and **fore**.

The rear foot consists of the **subtalar joint** and the **calcaneum**. This area is extremely important for runners, as it determines how the foot will land.

The midfoot is the arch of the foot and absorbs a lot of stress. It consists of five bones: the **cuboid**, **navicular** and three **cuneiforms**.

The forefoot consists of the long toe bones, called **metatarsals**, **tarsals** and **phalanges**.

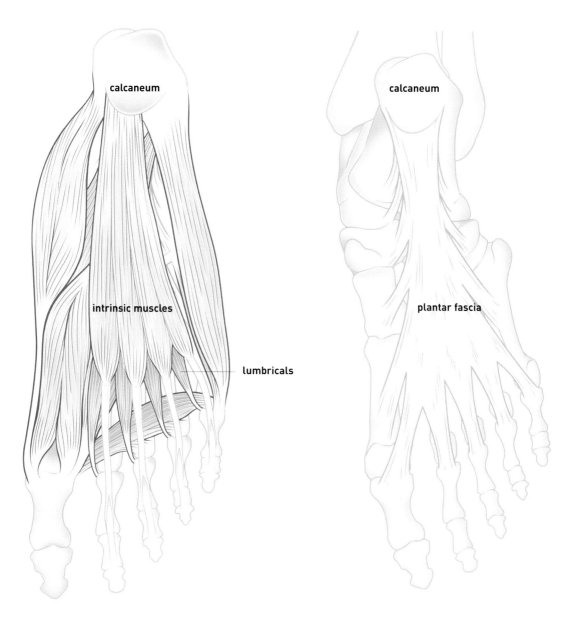

calcaneum

intrinsic muscles

lumbricals

calcaneum

plantar fascia

Sole of foot

The foot has an intricate network of small muscles, the **intrinsics** and **lumbricals**, that help keep its shape.

Many tendons run under the foot, supporting the arch and working the toes from the leg.

The **sinus tarsi tunnel** (see opposite) can cause chronic lateral ankle pain in runners who overpronate.

The heel is connected to the forefoot via a long ligament, the **plantar fascia**, which is pulled tight during the gait cycle to load the foot.

foot and ankle pain symptoms map (see note on page 115)

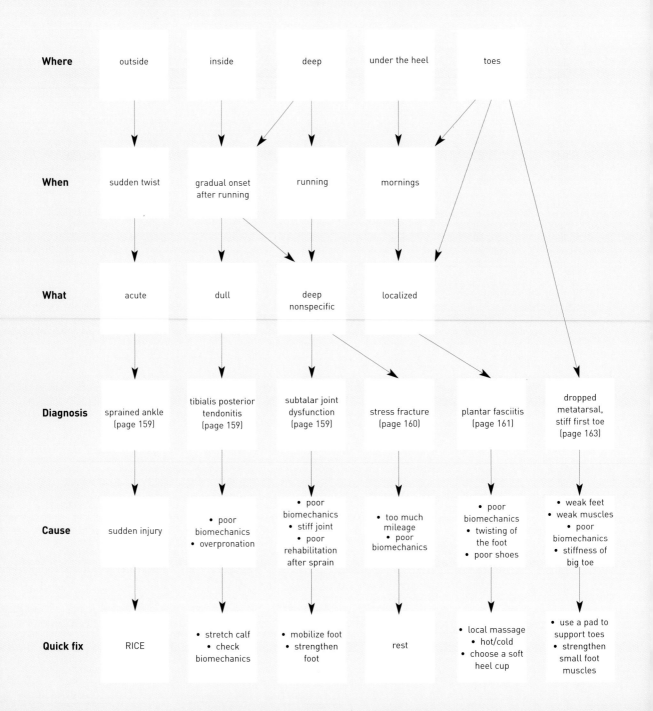

Where	outside	inside	deep	under the heel	toes
When	sudden twist	gradual onset after running	running	mornings	
What	acute	dull	deep nonspecific	localized	
Diagnosis	sprained ankle (page 159)	tibialis posterior tendonitis (page 159)	subtalar joint dysfunction (page 159)	stress fracture (page 160)	plantar fasciitis (page 161)	dropped metatarsal, stiff first toe (page 163)
Cause	sudden injury	• poor biomechanics • overpronation	• poor biomechanics • stiff joint • poor rehabilitation after sprain	• too much mileage • poor biomechanics	• poor biomechanics • twisting of the foot • poor shoes	• weak feet • weak muscles • poor biomechanics • stiffness of big toe
Quick fix	RICE	• stretch calf • check biomechanics	• mobilize foot • strengthen foot	rest	• local massage • hot/cold • choose a soft heel cup	• use a pad to support toes • strengthen small foot muscles

Sprained ankle

The most common ankle injury – in fact the most common sports injury of all – is an acute sprained ankle, which happens when the ankle twists too far, such as on uneven terrain or off a curb. There will be immediate pain and swelling, and you won't be able to carry on running; if it's very severe, any kind of weight-bearing will be painful. The most common sprain is an inversion injury, which damages the structures on the outside of the joint (the lateral ligaments). It is much harder to sprain the more stable medial side.

What to do
Immediate RICE will help a speedier recovery of the sprained ankle. Take the shortest route home and ice immediately. A grade one sprain settles quickly with a couple of days rest, but a grade two sprain requires more attention. After 48 hours, start with gentle mobility exercises, taking the joint forward and back and rotating it. Once walking is pain free, gentle balance exercises can begin. Try standing on one leg at first, then try it while shutting your eyes, and then try catching a ball (with your eyes open again!). A wobble board or minitrampoline may also be used. It is really important after a sprain to prevent the ankle from stiffening up, as this will result in altered biomechanics and possible further injury.

If a sprained ankle hasn't settled after four to six weeks, further investigation is recommended, as you could have a bone injury. If there is intense pain upon pressing of the malleolus, an x-ray is required, in case a bony injury has been missed. Alternatively, it could be a bone bruise to the head of the talus.

Tibialis posterior tendonitis

Pain on the inside of the ankle joint is more likely to be an overuse problem, called tibialis posterior tendonitis, than a sprain. This involves inflammation of the tibialis posterior tendon as it winds under the medial malleolus. It will hurt to palpate the tendon during and after running (particularly on push-off), and there will be stiffness in the morning, sometimes accompanied by swelling and creaking locally.

The possible causes are similar to those of MTSS (see page 153) – overpronation, a weak tibialis posterior muscle or a stiff ankle joint, following a sprain or fracture.

What to do
Rest immediately, as this can quickly become a chronic and persistent problem. Start stretching the calf and tibialis posterior muscles (see page 38), use ice and anti-inflammatories and wait to see if the symptoms settle. If they don't, get help in mobilizing the area and have your biomechanics assessed. Finally, check that the subtalar joint is mobile (see page 160).

Other tendinopathies

There are two less common tendinopathies around the ankle. Pain on the outside of the joint is usually caused by peroneal tendinopathy, which can occur as a result of running on excessive slants or slopes. Pain over the front of the joint may be caused by irritation of the tibialis anterior tendon, which lifts the foot. This can result from too much downhill running – or downhill running with poor technique.

What to do
Modify your training – eliminating the likely cause – to allow the inflammation to settle. Take some anti-inflammatories and use ice after training, or twice daily if you aren't able to run.

Subtalar joint dysfunction/sinus tarsi syndrome

The subtalar is part of the rear foot: it is the joint between the heel bone and the talus. If the joint is stiff, the foot won't be able to evert (turn out at the heel) properly. This will result in more pronation and torsion (rotation) of the foot and leg.

Inflammation in this area can cause sinus tarsi syndrome (STS), which manifests as lateral ankle pain just in front of the lateral ankle bone and as a pinching sensation – symptoms are often worse in the mornings. This can be one of those problems that gets diagnosed after a persistent irritation doesn't ease.

The sinus tarsi tunnel sits between the talus and the calcaneum and holds some of the joint's stabilizing ligaments. STS can be secondary to a sprained ankle, or due to overpronation. The tissues within the tunnel become impinged and inflamed. There may be feelings of instability and pain to run, particularly on uneven surfaces or on the bends of a track.

What to do
If it hurts to run, cross-train and get the injury reviewed by a sports-injury specialist, who should also take a look at your running shoes. Anti-inflammatories and rest, combined with strengthening the joint and mobilizing the subtalar joint (see right), should help. An anti-inflammatory injection is an option if the problem is not settling.

Do some single-leg balance work and strengthen the tibialis posterior muscle to prevent overpronation (see position b of the calf stretch exercise on page 38).

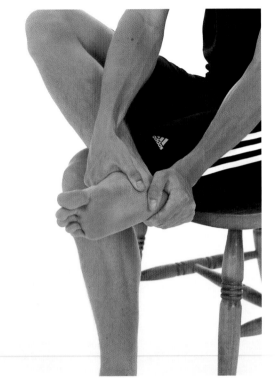

Mobilizing the subtalar joint
Cross the ankle over one knee while in a sitting position and take hold of the inside of the heel bone. Try to glide it down toward the floor, keeping the leg still with the other hand. Repeat 20 times.

Test both feet and see if you detect more stiffness in one than the other.

SARAH'S CASEBOOK

I treated a runner who had a stress fracture of the second toe. She rested for six weeks, then returned to training. After approximately four weeks she did a track session and two races in one week. This was too much for the healing bone and she had to have a further six weeks rest. So remember, when you are returning to exercise after injury: caution and patience pay off.

Stress fractures
Stress fractures commonly occur in the metatarsals and the navicular, and less commonly in the talus and the calcaneum. The second metatarsal is the most common site in runners and can be due to stiffness in the forefoot and big toe. A stress fracture to the navicular manifests as pain just in front of the medial malleolus and in the metatarsals, the long toe bones. It normally hurts to touch and on weight-bearing exercises, like hopping and running. The cause is usually chronic repetition of movement with

incorrect biomechanics, especially overpronation, although if the pain is more lateral, excessive supination may be the cause. Stress fractures can also result from a sudden increase in training volume.

What to do
Rest the area immediately if a stress fracture is suspected. At the start of a stress fracture – known as a stress response – just two weeks of rest and cross-training may be enough to prevent the problem from getting worse. While you are resting, strengthen the small muscles of the foot: ballerinas have to do this as a matter of course, and they do thousands at a time! Try the exercises below, gradually increasing the number each time.

If there is a more serious stress fracture, and more of the bone is involved, you may need 6 to 12 weeks of

rest. If the damaged area is the talus or navicular, you may be put into a cast, as these don't tend to heal as easily.

Plantar fasciitis

Plantar fasciitis is pain under the heel where the long ligament of the foot pulls on the bottom part of the calcaneum, the heel bone, which is covered by a fleshy fat pad. Plantar fasciitis can be caused by excessive twisting in the foot (resulting from overpronation), a stiff foot and ankle, tight calf muscles or weak foot muscles.

Worn trainers, resulting in repeated heel strike with no cushioning, or trainers with a soft forefoot allowing excessive toe bending, are other possible causes of this condition.

Foot-strengthening exercises
Start with the foot on a towel on the floor and try to scrunch up the towel under the foot **(a)**, then try to lift the arch across the top of the toes, making a dome shape, and pull the toes up creating a space under the toes.

Next, try picking up a pencil with the toes **(b)** and, if you're really good, draw with it!

a

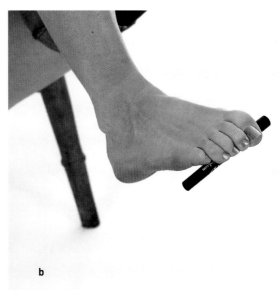

b

Pain is worse after periods of rest and especially in the morning, but then eases off, only to increase throughout the day with prolonged activity, especially in the push-off phase of running and walking.

What to do
Local massage using a golf ball and alternating immersion in hot and cold bowls of water will help. A soft heel cup may ease some of the discomfort of foot strike. Try to avoid walking barefoot.

Avoid running and stretching first thing in the morning, when everything is tighter, and if you continue to run, decrease the intensity of training until the condition settles. If you get pain on running that doesn't go away, rest and follow the advice here to let it settle.

As with the Achilles tendon, problems with the plantar fascia are thought to be degenerative and not inflammatory, so avoid any anti-inflammatory injections in this area, which have been strongly associated with ruptures of the plantar fascia.

Start stretching the foot gently on a slope and, as the pain decreases, add a stretch of the toes, using a resistance band to lift the toes while stretching the arch of the foot. Mobilize the sciatic nerve in the

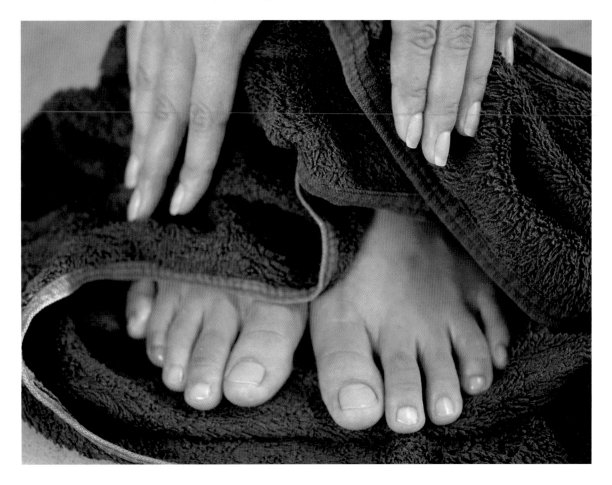

straight-leg position (see page 41) to ensure there are no neural adhesions, and stretch the calf muscles. Strengthen all the small foot muscles using the exercises on page 161. If the pain is very acute, taping or a night splint may help. Check your shoes – a stability or motion-control shoe that controls pronation may be necessary.

Pain in the big toe

The big toe, or first metatarsal, is a key area for runners, as it's the main pivot of the body. If it is stiff, the foot has to overpronate to compensate. Stiffness in the big toe is called hallux limitus or hallux rigidus, depending on how stiff it is. This can result from excessive pronation or just too much wear and tear over the years. The big toe can also become inflamed and red and start to turn in across the second toe, a condition commonly known as a bunion.

What to do

If the toe is red and inflamed, anti-inflammatories and ice will help. Try to mobilize the toe if it is stiff by flexing and extending it manually and rotating it around in both directions. Orthotics can help by allowing the toe to drop and roll forward without overpronating. Surgery may be the only solution for bunions that become really inflamed and painful.

Dropped metatarsal heads

The metatarsal heads are the joints that run across the foot at the same level as the ball of the big toe. Sometimes, these can drop and cause pain. It can feel as though you are walking on bone. With this condition, you can see the affected joint sitting below the others if you look at the foot, and you will occasionally feel it protruding underneath.

What to do

A cushioned pad under the metatarsal heads can lift the joints and ease pain. Known as a metatarsal head support, this is available from most good drugstores. The small muscles under the foot will need strengthening to support the joints (see page 161). It is fine to run if using the pad enables you to do so pain-free. Once there is no pain when walking with bare feet, you can try running without the pad, but if the pain returns, continue to use it. It is worth trying to stretch some of the tight joint structures across the top of the foot, too: take hold of the toes and bend them under, concentrating on the painful joint.

Morton's neuroma

Morton's neuroma is pain and inflammation of the nerve running between the toes and is extremely painful when the toes are squeezed together. This can sometimes occur alongside a stress fracture. It's most common between the third and fourth metatarsals and can be due to overtight shoes or laces.

What to do

Again, a metatarsal pad may help, and a local anti-inflammatory injection can help to settle the pain. You may also need to consider getting orthotics if the problem persists.

chapter 11

back on track

returning to running after injury, illness, pregnancy – or just a little time off

We all have times – forced or unforced – when we stop running. And whatever the cause of your break, it's crucial that when you get back to running, you do it sensibly and cautiously. Remember the principles of progressive overload and reversibility? The body likes training to be regular and consistent – and it doesn't like being thrown in at the deep end after time off. In fact, try to pick up where you left off after an injury, and you'll probably end up straight back in the sports-injury clinic.

What have I lost?

How much fitness you lose as a result of your break from running depends on whether you have managed to do any cross-training and the length of time you've been out for. Research shows that a two- to four-week period of complete inactivity results in:

● A decrease in VO_2max (the amount of oxygen you can extract from the air and use in the working tissues) of 4–10 percent.
● A reduction in blood volume.
● A reduction in stroke volume (the volume of blood pumped out of the heart per beat).
● A decrease in lactate threshold.
● Loss of flexibility.
● Reduction in muscle glycogen levels.

To put this in perspective, a 40-minute 10K runner could expect to add one to two minutes to their time after a three-week break. But bear in mind that these physiological declines begin to take place only after one to two weeks without training – not within the first few days – and also that we are talking here about complete inactivity. Studies have shown that if you decrease only the volume of training (the overall time or distance, rather than the intensity), aerobic conditioning can be maintained for up to 15 weeks. And that's where those cross-training sessions come in. Research suggests that keeping your heart rate above 70 percent of maximum during cross-training will enable you successfully to maintain your fitness. See chapter 8 for more details.

Returning from injury

There's a theory that runners go through a five-stage process when they get injured, starting with denial, then anger, bargaining, depression and acceptance. Sarah's experience in the clinic lends support to this theory and suggests that progress can really be made only once a runner reaches the stage of acceptance. Acceptance doesn't mean resignation: it simply means being realistic about your injury and its consequences. Then you are willing to stop risking doing yourself further harm by continuing to run, you understand that you have to readjust your goals, and you're ready to be fully engaged in the rehabilitation process.

Do try to keep a positive outlook during your injury time – and help others who are injured to do the same. Try to keep injured running buddies positive and involved, and support them as much as you can. Encourage them to accompany you on the bike while you are running, for example. Research shows that optimists deal with injury better, don't feel that the injury is their fault, have a belief that the problem will heal – and recover much more quickly.

That's not to say they rush through the recovery process, however. It's a good idea to break down the recovery process into small steps, with realistic mini-goals to achieve as you climb up to each level. Trying to go back before you are ready is the biggest cause of reinjury.

Fear of reinjury

Secretly, we all think we are invincible. So an injury is both a physical and a mental blow – and is often accompanied by fear of reinjury. That's why it is so important to get the right advice: then you can feel confident that the cause of your injury has been correctly identified. That's also why it's so important that you have faithfully followed your rehabilitation program. If you haven't, you may be prone to reinjuring the same area or more likely to injure something else. Getting expert advice is one thing, but following it is quite another and something that is in only your hands.

Getting ready to run

How do you know when you're ready to get back to running? An absence of pain is one of the most obvious signs – not just when walking and during everyday activities, but also when you are stressing the previously injured area. For example, you should be able to hop pain-free on a rehabilitated sprained ankle.

Don't be in denial about your recovery. If you still have pain, or limited function, you are not ready to get back to running yet and doing so is foolhardy. Continue with pain-free cross-training and treatment from a sports-medicine expert.

If you are fully pain-free, you are ready to begin your return to running – turn to chapter 11. It's a good idea to continue with some cross-training initially: you can make the cross-training sessions your tough ones so you don't have to worry that you are overstretching

ARE YOU INJURY PRONE?

Certain personality factors, attitudes and stress levels have a part to play in your risk of injury. A study in the *Journal of Personality and Social Psychology* found that the people most likely to have to take time off their sport because of injury were those with increased life stress, little social support and poor coping skills.

Extreme anxiety about your impending performance in a race (or even a training session) can raise your injury risk, too. If you are highly stressed (known as being in a heightened state of arousal), your heart rate will be elevated, your concentration diminished and muscular tension increased, causing altered motor patterns and loss of rhythm. That said, some runners cope very well with stress and actually need the adrenaline to get psyched up for a race.

yourself with running. As a rule, it takes two weeks to get back every week of running lost through injury, so don't expect to go straight back to where you were.

Don't be impatient, or try to cut corners. You need to reassess your goals, put races on hold and accept that you won't be running personal bests immediately. Try running without a watch or heart-rate monitor to prevent obsessing over slower times and higher heart rates.

Returning from illness

Illness can be the bane of a runner's life. You're in great shape, you're not injured and then BANG! You get a stinking cold a week before your big race. Are runners more susceptible to coughs, colds and flu? There is some evidence that a long, hard session lowers immunity temporarily for up to nine hours. That's why it's important to practice good rest and recovery habits. However, moderate running – and the health benefits it brings – actually boosts the immune system, enabling your body to fight disease more effectively.

OVERTRAINING

If you are constantly tired, moody or irritable, or if your limbs feel heavy, you are suffering frequent illness, have lost your appetite, aren't sleeping well and are unable to perform to your expectations, you may have overtraining syndrome. This is accumulated fatigue, resulting from excessive training and inadequate recovery. Poor diet, particularly inadequate calorie intake, and insufficient carbohydrate and water consumption are other contributing factors. Many runners don't cater well to the demands that intensive training puts on the system and end up lacking energy for the next session. Review your training journal to see when these symptoms started and what the likely causes are. It may be worth a visit to your doctor for blood tests to check that there is no viral component. The first step is to decrease the volume and intensity of your training immediately. If this doesn't help, you may need a period of complete rest from running. Try easing off for a minimum of four weeks and see whether you regain your energy and enthusiasm for exercise. If your periods have stopped or become irregular, see your doctor, as you may be losing valuable bone density and putting your health at risk.

To run or not to run?

So how do you know if you should or shouldn't run when you are under the weather? An elevated resting heart rate is indicative of illness. If your usual resting heart rate is higher than normal by a few beats, proceed with caution. It's a good idea to check your resting pulse rate regularly as a matter of course. You should also perform the "neck check." If your symptoms are from the neck upward, such as a runny nose, watery eyes or a mild sore throat – give running a try. Reduce your distance and intensity, though – try to keep your heart rate below 70 percent of maximum. If you have a cough, a "heavy" chest, general aches or a fever, do not run. Running with a fever can inflame the heart and is downright dangerous.

Once you are on the road to recovery, you can use the same tests to determine whether you can start running again. If you've had a virus or a fever, it's wise to get the all-clear from your doctor. And, finally, use your common sense – allowing yourself time to get back gradually to where you were before illness struck.

Getting back to running after pregnancy

Lots of elite runners, such as Ingrid Kristiansen and Sonia O'Sullivan, famously started running again shortly after having their babies, only to end up surpassing their previous performance. But what about you? Well, a lot depends on what you did before you were pregnant and what you were able to do during your pregnancy. Factors such as your previous fitness level, your pregnancy and the delivery itself will dictate your rate of progress.

For the first six weeks, it's best to stick with walking: this can be a lovely, bonding time for you and the baby out in the buggy. As a general rule, if you had a normal vaginal delivery, you should be ready to run after your six-week check with the doctor, provided there is no more bleeding. But remember, everyone is different, so don't feel pressured to start if you don't feel ready; and if you really feel fine, you may want to try a gentle jog earlier. If you have had a caesarean, you'll need to wait until the consultant gives you the all-clear to run. It certainly won't be within the first six weeks, as you have had major abdominal surgery and will need more time for healing and recovery – up to six months is usual.

Once you've had the all-clear from your doctor, you can start adding some short bouts of running to the walking. Take six weeks to build up to 30 minutes of running, gradually increasing the amount of time spent running and reducing the amount of time spent walking. The level 1 program opposite is a good place to start. Also bear in mind the following advice:

● Make sure you get plenty of rest and keep well hydrated, especially if you are breastfeeding.

● Keep your expectations low: you are trying to adapt to life with a new baby as well as run! Accept any help that comes along.

● Be flexible – the baby will probably dictate when you can run.

● Just enjoy the first three months of running, and don't look at pace or times.

● Ensure you do all the recommended postnatal exercises, especially the pelvic floor and abdominal exercises. Your body has been through a lot and won't be as strong as before. Remember that your ligaments will stay lax for up to six months after breastfeeding has stopped, so you may also be more injury prone – another reason to take it easy.

Back in the running

The following three programs are designed to ease runners of all levels of experience back into running after a break. They offer a good guide as to how fast you should progress, but remember that there are no hard-and-fast rules – and it's important not just to listen to your body, but to respect its needs, too.

Level 1 is a walk/run program, suitable for runners who did a little running before they got injured or had time out. It's also suitable for new moms. If you've had a sustained period out of the sport and have not run for more than three months with no other form of cross-training, you should also start here.

Level 2 is an easy running program, designed for the fit recreational runner who has been out of running for six weeks or so with an injury, illness or otherwise, but who has managed to do some cross-training and not lost too much aerobic conditioning.

Level 3 is suitable for experienced runners who have managed to maintain their fitness through cross-training during their break from running. If this sounds like you, but you've had a longer lay off – longer than 12 weeks, for example – precede this program with the Level 2 regimen.

Level 1 program
Week 1
Walk for 20 minutes every other day.

Week 2
Walk for 10 minutes to warm up, then add 2 minutes jog plus 2 minutes walk for 10 minutes, with 5 minutes walk to cool down. Aim to do this three or four times per week.

Week 3
Walk for 10 minutes to warm up, then increase
the time running to 4 minutes with 2 minutes walk
recovery. Repeat this three times, then walk for
5 minutes to cool down. Aim to do this three or
four times per week.

Week 4
Same as week 3, but try three 5-minute runs with a
1-minute walk recovery.

Week 5
Now try four 5-minute runs with a 1-minute walk
recovery or, if you feel able, do two 10-minute runs.
Aim to do this three to four times per week.

Week 6
You should now be able to jog for 20 minutes without
stopping. Aim to do this three or four times per week.

To progress, increase your running time or mileage
by no more than 10 percent per week. Once you are
comfortable with steady running for 30–40 minutes,
you can begin to increase your pace, or include some
faster intervals.

Level 2 program
Week 1
5 minutes walk to warm up, then 10 minutes jog and
5 minutes walk cool-down. Try to do this three to four
times per week.

Week 2
5 minutes walk to warm up, then 12 minutes jog.
Increase each run by 2 minutes if there is no reaction.
Aim for three to four sessions per week.

Week 3
Sustain 20 minutes of running. Try to do this four
times this week.

Week 4
If there has been no adverse reaction to 20 minute
runs, start to increase each run by 2 minutes, four
times per week.

Week 5
You should now be able to run for 30 minutes without
any adverse reaction. Do not exceed five sessions
per week.

Week 6
You can now start increasing your pace, but don't
increase your running time past 30 minutes. Start
with a 10-minute jog warm-up, then do five 2-minute
faster efforts (but not maximal), then a 10-minute jog
cool-down. Alternate this session with a 30-minute
easy run.

To progress, remember the 10 percent rule for
increasing distance or time spent running – and don't
increase more than one variable (such as both time
and pace) at once.

Level 3 program
Week 1
Start with 10 minutes easy jogging on alternate days.
If there is no adverse reaction or fatigue, gradually
increase the time by 3 minutes per session.

Week 2
Start running two days on and one day off. The time
can be gradually increased in the same 3-minute
intervals. By the end of week 2 you could be running
30 minutes at an easy pace.

Week 3
Stay with two days on and one day off. Don't increase
the time that you run for, but gradually increase the
speed of the running so you maintain an even pace
for 30 minutes.

Week 4

Alternate three sessions this week. For the first, do a 10-minute jog warm-up, 10-minutes at an increased pace and then a 10-minute jog cool-down. For the second session, go back to an easy jog for 30 minutes. Have a rest day. For the final session, do a 10-minute jog warm-up, five 2-minute efforts, then a 10-minute jog cool-down.

Weeks 5 and 6

Continue with the sessions described for week 4, adding one further session, if you feel able, so that you are running for three days and then having a rest day. This means you are now able to run six times per week, include specific types of sessions and are ready to get back into full training.

Once you are fully back on track, increase your training mileage by only 10 percent at a time. Listen to your body and make sure you take plenty of rest.

chapter 12

first aid

prevention and treatment of
common running ailments and annoyances

Not all the afflictions that we runners face are injuries, and while something as trivial as a blister or stomach cramp shouldn't put you out of action, it's good to know how best to deal with such irritations.

Foot problems

We put our feet through a lot as runners and don't give them much thanks for all their hard work. It is a myth that you should "harden up" your feet for running. Keeping them soft and supple is far less likely to result in blisters and calluses. Use a pumice stone or foot file to soften any hardened patches, particularly on the edge of the big toe and the joint below it, and moisturize regularly.

Athlete's foot

Athlete's foot is a fungal infection that thrives in damp, sweaty places, like between your toes. Minimize the risks by always washing and drying between your toes and making sure feet are completely dry before putting on socks. Wear flip-flops when you are in public wet areas, such as shower blocks or gym changing rooms. If you do get infected, use an antifungal product, such as Lamisil – and remember to treat your trainers too, as they may be harboring the fungus. Tea tree oil can be an effective treatment: dab over the affected area. If you are prone to athlete's foot, it's worth stocking up on, as it can also be used as a preventative measure.

Blisters and corns

Blisters are caused by repetitive friction on a specific point of the foot resulting in a build-up of fluid between the upper and lower layers of the skin. People who sweat a lot tend to be more prone to blisters, but often the problem causing both blisters and corns is poorly fitting socks or shoes. See the lacing techniques on pages 48–49 to ensure your shoes aren't slipping, wear flat-seamed or seamless socks (double-layered ones work well for blister sufferers) and protect vulnerable areas of skin with lubricant such as petroleum jelly (one school of thought), or moleskin or surgical tape (the other school of thought).

If you get a blister, protect it from further friction with a "second skin" style blister pad, such as Dr. Scholl's. Pop a blister only if it feels painful. If you do opt to pop, use a needle sterilized in a flame or boiling water, and puncture it close to the unblistered skin to drain the fluid. Dab antiseptic lotion on the area, and then cover with a blister pad for at least 48 hours before leaving bare. Always stop to deal with a developing blister problem rather than running through it – keep a stash of pads handy.

Corns form when there is excessive pressure on a particular area of skin, causing a build-up of the squamus layer. They are best removed professionally with a scalpel. Then protect the area with a corn cushion. But remember to treat the cause to stop corns forming in the first place. To prevent further corns occurring, use a layer of petroleum jelly over the corn and on the outside of the sock.

Black toenails

More properly known as subungual hematoma (that'll impress your running buddies!), black toenails occur when the shoe is too tight or when the big (or longest) toe makes too much contact with the end of the shoe, causing the nail to be pushed down into the nail bed, which becomes inflamed and bruised. If there is a painful build-up of blood under the nail, you can alleviate it by putting a sterile needle (heated in a flame) in the nail and releasing the pressure underneath. Sarah won her husband's heart by doing this on their first date, enabling him to play soccer!

If you aren't this brave, your doctor can do it for you. To minimize the risk of it happening in the first place – and prevent ingrowing toenails – cut nails short and straight across, and make sure shoes fit properly.

Gastrointestinal problems

According to one study, 83 percent of marathon runners said they occasionally or frequently suffered from what we politely refer to as gastrointestinal (GI) disturbances – anything from gripping stomach pains to nausea and diarrhea. Women appear to suffer more than men, but both sexes are more vulnerable during or after tougher running sessions.

Finding the cause of your specific problem is usually a case of trial and error, because no single factor has been found to be the culprit in all cases of GI disturbance. It could be related to the content and timing of your meals, hydration levels, fatigue, reduced blood flow to the digestive system, alcohol or caffeine consumption, or even medication.

Stitch
Scientists have coined an impressive name for the stitch – exercise-related transient abdominal pain (ETAP) – but they still haven't really figured out what it is or how to get rid of it. While stitches are common among runners, they aren't exclusive to them, which puts paid to the idea that it's all the jolting around of the internal organs that causes a stitch. So what are the theories? Some research suggests that a lack of oxygen supply to the diaphragm muscle (the dome-shaped muscle that sits below the lungs) is the likely cause, while other studies implicate stress on the visceral ligaments (the ones that keep everything in place inside the abdominal cavity).

The most recent research, from Australia, suggests that stitches could be caused by irritation of the peritoneum, a double-layered membrane that

surrounds the abdominal cavity. The fact that stitches are most prevalent in sports that involve repetitive torso movement led the researchers to investigate this idea. The outer layer, the parietal peritoneum, lies closest to the abdominal muscles and attaches to the abdominal wall, while the inner layer, the visceral peritoneum, is wrapped around the internal organs. Between the two membranes is a fluid-filled space – the peritoneal cavity – which allows them to slide freely over each other. The theory is that the parietal peritoneum becomes irritated, either because the amount of fluid between the two membranes is reduced as a result of blood flow being directed to the working muscles, or because of a distended stomach pushing the inner surface against it. The result? That gripping pain in your side.

The same Australian researchers also found that 14 percent of stitch sufferers experienced shoulder-tip pain. A strange coincidence? Probably not. They believe that shoulder-tip pain may be a result of referred pain, as the phrenic nerve, which runs down to the diaphragm, originates from the same place as the nerve supplying the shoulder.

Stitch avoidance
● Avoid eating a full meal one to two hours before a run – research found this increased the incidence of stitches in participants of a mass running event.
● Experiment with different breathing techniques. Belly breathing (where you inflate the belly as you inhale and draw it in as you exhale) can help.
● Drink little and often when running, not large volumes of fluid at once (which will distend the stomach). And think about what you drink. In one study, researchers examined the effect of different fluids and the likelihood of getting a stitch. Fruit juice was least well tolerated, increasing the incidence of stitches and bloating. Its high carbohydrate content was believed to be the reason, which is why it's important to ensure that if you drink something other

than water, it is an isotonic drink (6–8 percent carbohydrate solution) and not one with a higher carbohydrate concentration.

● Don't skimp on your warm-up: in a survey, runners believed this was a possible cause of their stitch pain.

● Strengthen your core muscles to support the abdominal contents adequately.

It seems that the prevalence and severity of stitches drops with age, if that's any consolation!

The runner's trots

While the jolting action of running may not be implicated in a stitch, it is almost certainly a contributing factor to the dreaded runner's trots, broadly defined as an urgent need to have a bowel movement, stomach cramps, loose stools or diarrhea. Add to that the fact that the flow of blood to the gastrointestinal tract is diverted to your legs during running and it's easy to see why this is such a widespread problem.

If you always get the urge "to go" a short time after starting to run, try keeping track of what you eat and drink, what time of day you suffer from the problem and when you have a bowel movement. It may be that simply shifting your run to a different time of day will solve matters. Many runners swear by having a cup of coffee before a run: this usually stimulates the bowels into action. However, caffeine and alcohol are known irritants of the stomach lining, so try not to drink too much of either if you are prone to stomach problems. As in the case of stitches, the high sugar content of sports drinks can also be a factor. Make sure your sports drink is only 6–8 percent carbohydrate. If you find that even this causes problems, you could experiment with diluting it with extra water. And always carry some toilet paper!

Avoiding the trots

● Try to eat at least two hours before you run – the presence of food in the stomach can make things worse.

● Experiment with avoiding high-fiber foods and dairy products close to a run.

● Drink plenty of fluids. Making yourself dehydrated won't help and, in fact, slows the body's ability to digest foods.

● If you have a crucial training session or race and are worried about your bowels misbehaving, consider taking an over-the-counter antidiarrheal as a precautionary measure.

● Avoid using aspirin, ibuprofen or other non-steroidal anti-inflammatories, which can cause gastrointestinal irritation.

● Be aware that large doses of vitamin C can cause diarrhea.

Muscle cramps

Here's another condition that scientists haven't got to the bottom of yet: muscle cramps, which nearly 70 percent of runners suffer from at some point.

While dehydration and loss of electrolyte salts are often blamed (and are likely to be a contributing factor), a study from the University of Alabama found that 69 percent of subjects suffered muscle cramps even when they were well hydrated and receiving electrolytes during workouts. And, in fact, too much water can also be a factor, as the extra sweating it triggers can expel essential salts from the body.

Some experts believe that bad posture or faulty biomechanics contribute to muscle cramps by overstimulating the Golgi tendon organs (those receptors in tendons that monitor muscular tension). This triggers a relaxation response in the relevant muscle and a simultaneous contraction in the opposing muscle, resulting in cramping.

Another theory relates to insufficient carbohydrate storage, resulting in the use of protein as a fuel. One study found that muscle cramps most commonly occurred in subjects with the highest levels of ammonia production (a sign of protein usage). So forget those low-carb diets!

Cramping is most common in muscles that cross more than one joint, such as the gastrocnemius muscle in the calf, which crosses the ankle and knee, and the biceps femoris, which crosses the hip and knee. According to research from Cape Town University in South Africa, stretching the offending muscle is one of the best solutions.

Cramp avoidance
● Stretch regularly, particularly focusing on the muscles prone to cramping.
● Stay well hydrated. If exercising in a hot or humid environment, ensure you keep fluid and electrolyte levels topped off by drinking a sports drink. Also use sports drinks in preference to water on your longer runs. In the Alabama study, cramp sufferers were able to exercise nearly twice as long before getting cramps when they drank a carbohydrate–electrolyte drink.
● Work on correcting any muscle imbalances or faulty biomechanics.
● Ensure your diet contains enough carbohydrate, potassium, magnesium and calcium. Sodium (salt) is also important in preventing cramps, but deficiencies in the Western diet are unlikely and sports drinks normally contain some sodium.
● Don't warm up too long before a race: if the body heats up and then rapidly cools, muscle cramps can result.

Urinary leakage

Urinary leakage or incontinence affects as many as 50 percent of women, particularly after pregnancy, and can really hamper running. It's usually caused by pelvic floor weakness as a result of misuse, disease or damage – and anything from sneezing to tripping over a pothole can result in urinary leakage.

The primary course of action is to do pelvic floor exercises, and lots of them. Providing they are done correctly, these exercises are 90 percent effective in stopping urinary incontinence. Often, when people say they don't work, it is because they have done far too few of them to make a difference, or done them incorrectly.

So what's the correct way? Sit, stand or lie with your legs slightly apart and your buttocks, abdominals and thighs relaxed. Now pull "up and in" as if you were trying to stop yourself from urinating (don't literally do this on the toilet, however, or you may cause a urinary tract infection). Breathing normally, continue to pull up and in through the vagina and the anus. The most common mistakes are to pull in the stomach or clench the buttocks. Make sure you are doing neither. Build up to 10 x 10 second holds.

Once you think you've got the hang of that, try the "lift" exercise. Draw the pelvic floor muscles up to the "first floor" and hold. Still breathing freely, now draw them up further, to the "second floor." As you get better at these, you can increase the height of the building and go up to the "third" or "fourth floor"! Mix both fast and slower contractions for best results and do these exercises as often as you can.

> **SARAH'S CASEBOOK**
> Use a prompt to remind you to do your pelvic floor exercises. Either set your watch to beep every few hours or put some stickers around the house – the fridge is a good place!

Overheating and dehydration

While dehydration can occur in the absence of overheating, the reverse is not true. When you are running in warmer temperatures – particularly if it's humid – you need to be extra vigilant about staying well hydrated and as cool as possible because of your increased sweat rate. That means wearing lightweight, breathable clothing, carrying fluids with you and protecting yourself with sunscreen, sunglasses and maybe a hat or visor.

It also means not expecting your body to react in the way it normally would. Research shows that even elite runners are 10 percent slower in hot conditions, and you can expect your heart rate to be higher for any given intensity of effort. If it is above 80°F and humid, it's best to avoid running until the day gets cooler, as your body is not efficient at cooling itself at temperatures this high.

It's possible, of course, to get dehydrated even on cooler days. You can read more about fluid intake on page 102, but suffice it to say there is evidence of a reduction in both mental and physical function even at low levels of dehydration, according to research from Loughborough University – including reduced alertness and ability to concentrate, tiredness, headache and poorer performance. Dehydration makes your blood thicken, reducing your heart's efficiency, increasing your heart rate and raising your body temperature. It can be extremely dangerous or even fatal. So, best avoided!

Avoiding overheating on the run
● Start off well hydrated.
● Run in cooler, shadier areas when possible.
● Run early in the morning or later in the evening when it's cooler.
● Carry fluid with you.
● Drink sports drinks.
● Spray or pour water over your head. Research

from the University of Birmingham found that this lowered perception of effort.

Hyponatremia

Literally translated as "low blood sodium," hyponatremia is caused by drinking too much water, lowering the concentration of sodium in the blood. In its mild form, hyponatremia can cause bloating and nausea or mental confusion; in extreme cases, it can lead to brain seizure and death. Incidences have increased in recent years, which many experts believe is a result of the constant "drink, drink, drink" message that runners are given. While it's important to stay well hydrated, you can have too much of a good thing. The current guidelines suggest drinking according to thirst and measuring body weight before and after a run to estimate fluid losses, rather than recommending a specific amount of fluid, wholesale, to everyone.

Hyponatremia is more common in women, because of their smaller body size and lower muscle mass, and slower runners tend to be more susceptible than faster ones, simply because they're out there running for longer periods and more at risk of taking on too much water.

Avoiding hyponatremia
● Drink little and often.
● Drink sports drinks rather than water on longer runs.
● Avoid using non-steroidal anti-inflammatories just before or during running. According to research from Baylor College of Medicine in Houston, these impair the body's ability to excrete water.
● Get accustomed to knowing how much fluid you need to feel comfortable and perform well.
● Check your urine. University of Connecticut researchers found that urine color correlated very accurately with hydration status. Pale yellow urine indicates you are within 1 percent of optimal hydration.

Skin problems

Chafing

The dreaded jogger's nipple, or indeed any area of chafing, can cause more pain than you'd think possible, whether it's soreness, dryness or full-on bleeding. Pick your clothes carefully (avoid cotton, which will hold on to sweat and make the garment cling) and take out any labels that rub. A lubricant, such as Bodyglide or Vaseline, can help reduce chafing, but if this doesn't help, you may need to put moleskin or a pad on any problem areas before you run, particularly for longer sessions.

Rash

A sweat rash under the arms, under the breasts or in the groin area is an unpleasant, but surprisingly common, running affliction. It's caused by a yeast that occurs naturally on the skin and which reacts with trapped sweat to cause a raised, red, often itchy and irritating rash. Minimize the risk by always showering immediately after running, not wearing dirty or overly tight clothing and by using lubricant to prevent chafing. If you do get a rash, treat it with an antifungal lotion or cream, preferably one combined with hydrocortisone, an anti-inflammatory, to reduce redness and itching.

Sunburn

A recent report from Austria suggested that marathon runners were more susceptible to skin cancer than non-marathon runners. Their sun exposure was markedly greater, as was the appearance of age spots or liver spots, which result from sun damage and are risk factors for melanoma. However, it may have been the runners' bad habits as much as their skin exposure that was to blame. Only half of them regularly used sunscreen and almost all of them exposed their legs, arms, shoulders and upper backs. The researchers suggest covering more skin and avoiding running in peak sunshine hours. Even if it is cloudy, don't forgo the sun protection – a great deal of the sun's rays still penetrate – and apply sunscreen 15 to 30 minutes before exposure.

Resources

Running clubs
To find a running club in your area, visit these sites:
Road Runners Club of America
www.rrca.org/clubs
Run The Planet
www.runtheplanet.com/resources/clubs
The Running Network
www.runningnetwork.com/clubs

Chi Running is a method that marries some of the principles of tai chi with a specific running technique.
www.chirunning.com

The Pose Method is Dr. Nicholas Romanov's system for teaching running technique and other movement.
www.posetech.com

The Art of Running is the name of Canadian coach Malcolm Balk's approach, which incorporates the Alexander Technique.
www.theartofrunning.com

Footwear
Adidas www.adidas.com
ASICS www.asics.com
Brooks www.brooksrunning.com
Inov-8 www.inov-8.com
Mizuno www.mizunousa.com
New Balance www.newbalance.com
Nike www.nike.com
Puma www.puma.com
Reebok www.rbk.com
Saucony www.saucony.com

The American Academy of Podiatric Sports Medicine website maintains an updated list of recommended running shoes.
www.aapsm.org

Runner's World magazine publishes comprehensive twice-yearly shoe reviews. Or look online in their Shoes & Gear section.
www.runnersworld.com

Specialist running stores
Fleet Feet Sports has more than 80 store locations throughout the US.
www.fleetfeetsports.com

Road Runner Sports has more than 20 store locations throughout the US and an online store.
www.roadrunnersports.com

Runner's World magazine features a store finder for specialty running stores on its website.
www.runnersworld.com/store/search

Sports injury contacts
American Physical Therapy Association
Find a qualified physical therapist in your area by visiting www.apta.org.

American Osteopathic Association
Find an osteopath in your area by visiting www.osteopathic.org.

American Chiropractic Association
Find a registered chiropractor in your area at www.amerchiro.org.

American Massage Therapy Association
Find a massage therapist in your area at www.amtamassage.org.

American Academy of Orthopaedic Surgeons
Find an orthopaedist in your area at www.aaos.org.

American Podiatric Medical Association
Find the nearest podiatrist in your area at www.apma.org.

American Orthopaedic Foot & Ankle Society
Find an orthopaedic foot and ankle specialist in your area at www.aofas.org.

The Virtual Sports Injury Clinic is an online resource featuring detailed information about sports-related injuries: www.sportsinjuryclinic.net.

Nutrition and hydration
Performance Food is a web-based service for athletes and sports people providing education and resources on nutrition to give optimal sports performance.
www.performancefood.co.uk

Gatorade Sports Science Institute provides articles, tips, research, educational tools, and interactive presentations on sports nutrition and exercise.
www.gssiweb.com

Training and rehabilitation aids
All manner of training aids, from exercise mats and wobble boards to flotation belts, resistance tubing, weights and Swiss balls are available from the following retailers:

Ideal Fitness
www.shapeupshop.com

Perform Better
www.performbetter.com

Amazon.com
www.amazon.com

Index

numbers in *italics* refer to illustrations